CW01498062

Insights into a Unique Business Model

Consulting Editor **David Barnes**

Consulting Editor
David Barnes

Managing director
Sian O'Neill

The Independent Bar: Insights into a Unique Business Model
is published by

Globe Law and Business Ltd
3 Mylor Close
Horsell
Woking
Surrey GU21 4DD
United Kingdom
Tel: +44 20 3745 4770
www.globelawandbusiness.com

The Independent Bar: Insights into a Unique Business Model

ISBN 9781787422520

Table of contents

Foreword

Chantal-Aimée Doerries QC
Atkin Chambers

This book is a must read for anyone involved in running or managing a barristers' chambers. It is surprising that this is the first book addressing the wide range of topics with which any manager of a barristers' chambers needs to be familiar. The breadth of topics covered, from marketing and media relations to international development, and from compliance and risk management to wellbeing, reflects how much the typical barristers' chambers has moved into the twenty-first century. The chambers' model or structure, through which the majority of barristers in England and Wales practise, very much meets the demands of the twenty-first century. It is lean, if properly run, in terms of overheads. It focuses on expertise and fosters excellence. It allows its members to adapt to the market, because the set-up allows for a flexibility with which few business models can compete. While a gig economy dominated by the outsourcing of almost every service undoubtedly has its challenges and limitations, the chambers' structure has, in a sense, at its heart, reflected the best aspects of this. Its members are independent and tend to work for limited periods for other lawyers or clients, whether providing advice or advocating on their behalf.

Management of chambers falls broadly into three areas, in no particular order: management and/or administration; development of business; and opportunities and responsibility, in the sense of responsibility for community within chambers and the community within which chambers sits. This book offers insight into each of these from real experts. Real in that the authors all have significant experience in grappling with and solving the challenges posed by chambers, as opposed to individuals with no experience of the Bar and chambers. That is part of what makes this book unique and very valuable to anyone working in, or considering working in, a barristers' chambers.

The chapters on "Strategy and why it is important", "Barristers' finance", "Compliance and risk management" and "Technology @ the Bar" provide a comprehensive guide to what it takes to run a chambers and address the particular challenges arising from running a business structure that consists of, and supports, many individual businesses within it. That is the peculiarity and the beauty of the structure – at its best it enables a diverse mix of specialists to practise as self-employed barristers under the umbrella of a chambers. It is a delicate balance between encouraging and promoting the individuality of each practitioner, while ensuring that the individuals function effectively and efficiently as a whole. Importantly, while the Bar remains at heart a profession, it has recognised that running a chambers requires an immense amount of professional and business skill. These chapters take the reader through the areas that a manager of barristers will need to understand.

The most visible changes affecting barristers' chambers have undoubtedly been in the way in which chambers present themselves to the outside world and how they attract work for their members. It is hard to believe that when I started in practice some 26 years ago, it was considered a little radical for a chambers to have a brochure. Chambers and their managers have rapidly adjusted to the new world, becoming adept at developing new opportunities. The chapters on "Practice management and business development", "International development", "Marketing and branding" and "Recruitment and talent management" focus on the issues which chambers and their managers need to consider and offer concrete advice on how to proceed. The Bar's continued success in attracting international work – earnings from international work have grown year on year for over a decade – is a sign of the profession's potential and the effectiveness of the chambers' structure.

A barristers' chambers is a community. This means that those of us in the community have a responsibility for others in the community. Accepting this responsibility is good from a business perspective, as well as, in some instances, being required by law and regulators. It is also the right thing to do. The "Wellbeing" chapter focuses on the steps the Bar has taken in recent years to foster discussion, raise awareness and to provide wellbeing support for all those working within the community. A number of senior clerks and heads of chambers shared individuals' stories with me during my time as Chair of the Bar, leaving me in no doubt that the pressures faced by professionals and those working in chambers have never been greater. We need to learn to be better at looking out for each other. While we have come a long way, diversity within the profession remains a challenge. The chapter on "Women in law" rightly notes that diversity is an asset and needs to be embraced. Cultural change remains necessary. This chapter looks at the progress we have made, but also highlights the continuing problems. Last, but by no means least, the "*Pro Bono*/CSR" chapter identifies the real and substantial commitment by the Bar to *pro bono* and offers useful guidance to those looking to do more.

In short, this book recognises the many challenges facing those responsible for the management of barristers' chambers, but it also paints a picture of a rewarding, interesting and varied world, and offers useful guidance to all those either involved in, or considering embarking on, a career in barristers' chambers.

Chantal-Aimée Doerries QC was called to the Bar 1992 and took silk in 2008. She specialises in UK and international commercial dispute resolution with particular expertise in disputes relating to energy and natural resources, infrastructure projects, joint ventures and commercial arbitration. She was the 2016 Chair of the Bar of England and Wales and has been head of Atkin Chambers since 2017.

Strategy and why it is important

Nicholas Luckman
Wilberforce Chambers

1. Introduction

The unprecedented change that the legal profession has seen over the past 10 years is only set to continue, and arguably at a much greater pace. The growth of digital technology, the forces of consolidation imposed by purchasers of legal services reducing panels, the breaking down of barriers to entry, and increased client power all serve to create more competition in an already highly competitive legal environment.

As the legal market becomes more distressed, only those with a strategy that creates value will be able to justify their place in the market and at the same time increase their prospects of survival. Barristers' chambers need to adapt to the changes in the way legal services are being supplied to meet the demands of the evolving legal market, and it may well be that simply relying on a high-quality, cost-effective legal resource is no longer sufficient on its own to guarantee success.

This chapter looks at why it is important to develop a vision and strategy, and considers how the chambers' business structure can achieve this, and at the same time add value and create sustainable competitive advantage. The focus of this chapter is on specialist commercial and chancery chambers, although the content is equally relevant to all chambers.

2. What is strategy and why does it matter?

The concept of strategy evolved from the Greek word '*strategia*' meaning the 'art of generalship or command', and has been taken from the military and adapted for business. There has been much discussion about what strategy actually means, and for those looking for an unambiguous 'one strategy fits all' definition to solve their business issues, they will be disappointed.

Michael Porter and Henry Mintzberg are two academics who have had the most influence in the study of strategy. Their contrasting views and approaches emphasise the different interpretations that strategy can have. Michael Porter[1] takes a more deliberate strategic approach, looking at cost leadership, market segmentation and differentiation to achieve strategic advantage, whereas Henry Mintzberg presents an emergent strategy where patterns in behaviour and learning what works in practice are central to creating strategic flexibility that can adapt to market variables to achieve strategic advantage. Both strategic approaches work, and indeed there are

---

1   Michael E Porter, *Competitive Advantage*, 1985, Ch 1, pp 11–15, The Free Press, New York.

many more adaptations such as the popular model of "Logical Incrementalism" introduced by James Quinn,[2] who suggests that strategy is developed logically through the unique needs of a business and managed incrementally to experiment and learn what works. The key is to choose a strategic approach that supports the culture of your business and fits the environment you operate in.

The legal environment gives chambers their means of survival, and whether it is in the context of the private or public sector, meeting clients' expectations and adding value should be central to the vision statement of any chambers. As can be seen from the approaches of Michael Porter and Henry Mintzberg, strategy does not set this vision of what a chambers wants to achieve or be; it is simply the means by which this vision or objective is met. Strategy for a chambers should therefore be a plan and a pattern of actions over time to achieve identifiable aims and objectives set out in its vision statement.

To help a chambers articulate its vision statement of business objectives and a plan of how to achieve them, a process of analysis, planning and implementation should be adopted. This is often referred to as a 'strategic management process' and identifies several areas that need to be addressed when working out what sort of chambers you want to be and then formulating a strategy to meet this vision. These areas are:

- understanding where you are as a chambers;
- understanding what you are good at and what you are not good at;
- understanding the culture of chambers;
- understanding the ambitions of members and staff;
- understanding what the future looks like;
- making choices about what to do and what not to do when developing a strategy route map for chambers; and
- implementing and turning the plans into reality.

I have adapted models (opposite and following page) from Johnson and Scholes' book *Exploring Corporate Strategy*[3] to help illustrate the cycle of analysis, planning and implementation. The first model shows the holistic strategic management process, and the second model illustrates the strategic analysis and planning stages of the process.

As can been seen from the models, this is a valuable process that helps a chambers to understand itself, the pressures it faces, and the vision and direction of travel to meet its aims.

With a strategy, chambers is better equipped to:

- create a vision and direction for the chambers where members and staff understand why they are doing things and what the common aims are. People deliver strategy, and reducing confusion and increasing understanding improves the prospect of success;
- understand its capabilities and core skills, where its weaknesses exist, and

2   JB Quinn, 1980, *Strategies for change: Logical incrementalism*, Homewood: Irwin.
3   G Johnson, K Scholes and R Whittington (2008), *Exploring corporate strategy*, Harlow: Prentice Hall.

Strategic management process

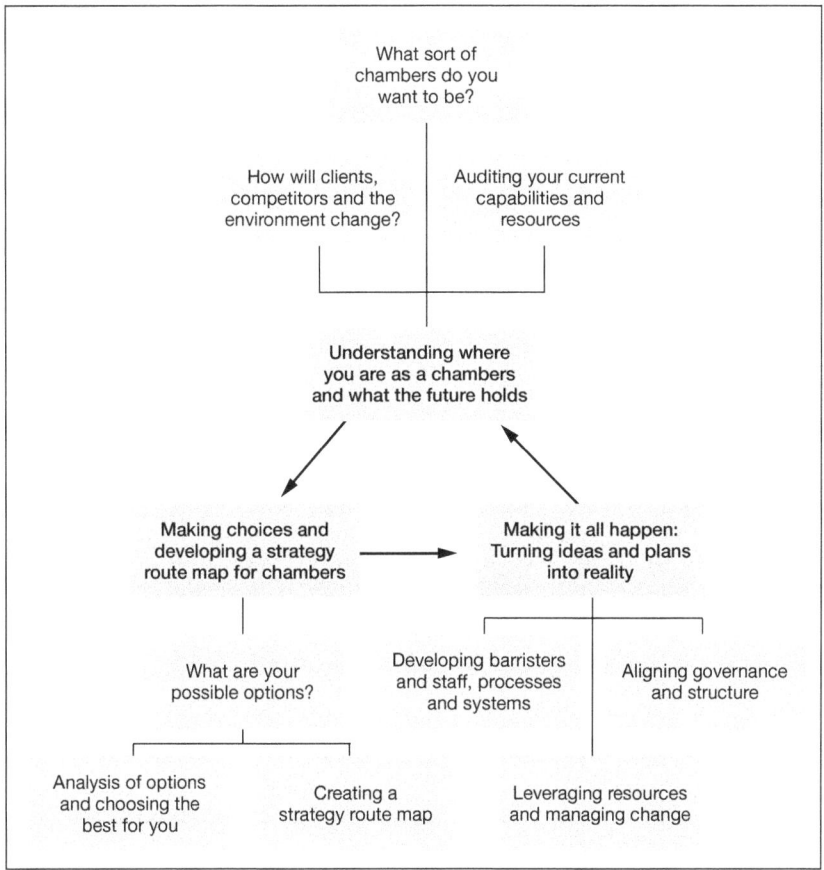

who its clients are. With this understanding, chambers can accurately decide whether it is supplying the right services, which markets support those services, and judge the correct timing of delivery;

- allocate and deploy scarce resources efficiently and where available use unique resources, such as a niche area of specialism, to underpin competitive advantage; and
- create sustainable competitive advantage by the way it positions itself to compete in the market in relation to key competitors. This involves chambers making the right decisions based on an understanding of its competitors, its markets, its special competencies and the opportunities and threats that exist.

Having a strategy matters and is fundamental to the success and sustainability of any chambers. Not having one, particularly in a time of market turbulence, increases the risk of failure.

Strategic management stage process

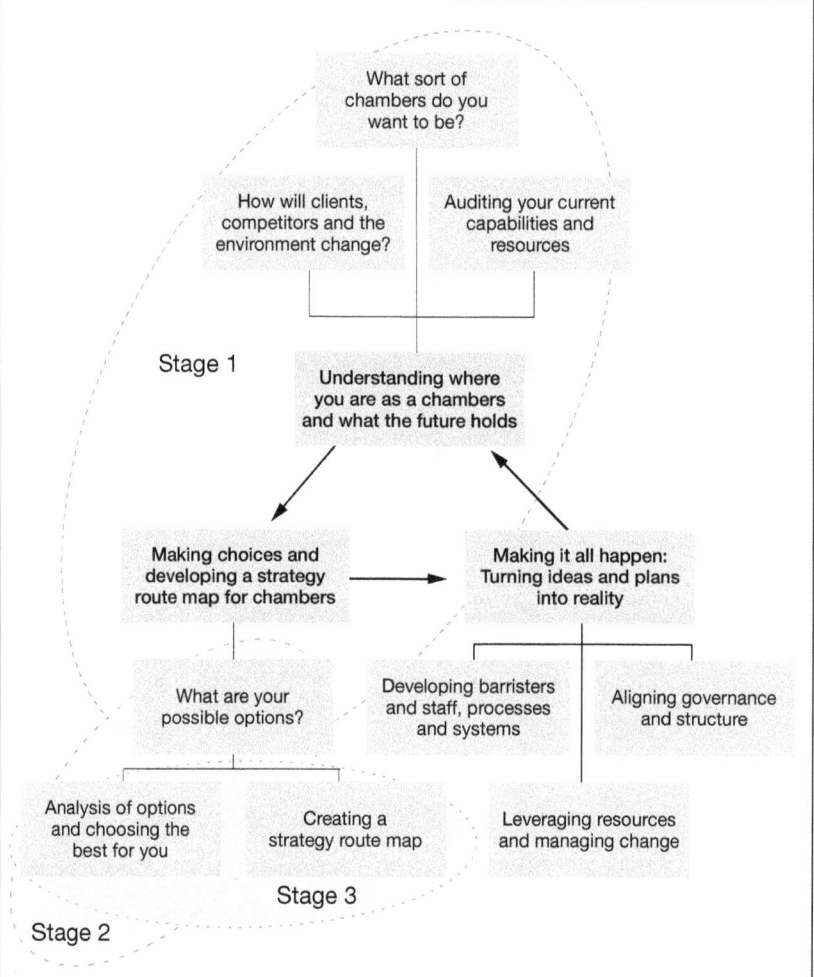

3. Key challenges for strategy development in a chambers

Strategy can only be given true effect through the actions of people, and it is therefore important that both barristers and staff understand the strategy and what chambers is trying to achieve.

Therefore, the key challenge for any chambers when developing and delivering a strategy is getting the buy-in and commitment from barristers and staff. To achieve this, the key areas that need to be aligned are structure, culture and leadership.

3.1 Structure and culture

The reason I have combined these areas is because the structure of any organisation is a consequence of its culture.

In the majority of cases the structure of a chambers can best be described as an unincorporated trade association of sole practitioners. When trading from a chambers, barristers share costs but not profit; and unlike law firms or most professional services structures, they are not partners.

The corporate governance framework of a chambers describing how the business is operated will be covered in a written constitution and supporting policies. These are drawn up to reflect whom the business is there to serve and who the stakeholders are, and to set out rules and a framework as to how the important issues regarding the running of chambers and its purpose are decided.

The power of decision-making is in the hands of the barristers and each member of chambers has an equal vote. In most chambers members will delegate authority to a management board or committee for day-to-day issues, but on important decisions, the constitution will usually provide for a full chambers vote and require a significant percentage or clear majority vote to carry a decision.

As mentioned above, structure is framed by culture, and most chambers have been structured in this way to support the culture of sole practitioners. With the right culture, where everyone involved understands the direction of chambers and shares the same ambitions and vision, this structure can provide for a dynamic and cohesive business with the majority of members involved in driving strategy that they believe in. However, with the wrong culture the equal vote structure does allow for strategic decisions to be frustrated by a minority.

The key structural challenge for strategic development in any chambers is the self-employed mindset of the barristers and an individualistic approach. Inevitably, self-interest for sole practitioners is difficult to suppress when they are making decisions that concern them, but this is why you need an identifiable strategy which is understood, achievable and adds value for the individual barristers as well as chambers as a whole. If barristers suspend self-interest and focus on the collective aims that they, their colleagues and the chambers are trying to achieve, this collaborative culture will drive strategy with far greater impact than an individual operating on their own is able to do.

So what is culture and why is it so important? The culture of a chambers is not formed overnight, it develops over time as individuals within chambers, both barristers and staff, gain experience through behaviour. This experience shapes the values, the beliefs and the way things are done by a chambers, known as an organisations culture.[4]

A chambers culture will largely be defined by observing the way it does things on a day-to-day basis. Such things might include regular events or rituals that it regards as important, the routine way members and staff behave both towards each other and externally, the committees and reporting channels that chambers uses as control systems, whether the chambers' structure supports everyone equally or allows influential members to exercise disproportionate power, and the style adopted when engaging with each other and clients. These are often described as a cultural mix of taken-for-granted assumptions about behaviour and actions within an organisation which shape its culture.

---

4   E Schein, *Organisation Culture and Leadership*, Jossey Bass, 1997.

When we are looking at strategy, unless we can understand the influence culture has on a chambers, it is difficult to assess how chambers will respond to any changes in strategy. It is therefore important to be able to characterise the culture of chambers and, as described by Charles Handy,[5] one way we can do this is by analysing the relationship between a chambers and individuals, and assessing how power and hierarchy are valued within a chambers environment. If you applied these criteria more generally, most chambers could be characterised as having a 'person culture', which is a culture where individuals put themselves before the organisation and regard their interests as primary. The danger with this is that the organisation takes a back seat and eventually suffers. This culture has the characteristics of self-interest, which historically has worked for chambers where the business decisions were reasonably straightforward. Chambers were much smaller and everyone knew each other, recruitment was largely limited to the pupillage process and nurturing new tenants, the flow of referral work from law firms was reasonably predictable and did not need strategic thought, and barristers made independent strategic career decisions when starting out based on a generic area of specialisation, such as chancery, commercial, family, common law or criminal law.

However, the challenging legal market that we have seen over the last few years is set to continue, and the uncertainty created by these challenges has been driving change. Chambers are becoming larger and more specialist, the chambers brand is increasingly valued by clients, the flow of work is less predictable, recruitment is a mixture of lateral hires and pupillage, talent management is about retention and development of each barrister, and service delivery involves increased levels of specialism, delivering added value and performing as part of a team. All of these drivers of change disrupt normal routine, which impacts on culture. Some chambers have reacted to this and have brought in experienced managers, senior clerks and CEOs to help manage these complex issues. Where these managers are allowed to take a lead role in developing a strategy to address these challenges there will inevitably be an impact on culture as it changes from a 'person' to a more 'power' culture, but if managed effectively and with support from members and staff, this should have a positive impact on delivering any agreed aims and objectives. However, where tension exists between the members and the senior manager over control of strategy, and as a consequence there is limited cooperation and collaboration, the risk that culture will defeat the strategic aims is much higher.

This raises the question of whether the 'person culture', with the characteristics of individuality and no single hierarchy, is capable of driving a strategy dealing with complex decisions in the current competitive legal environment. Arguably, some measure of leadership through a hierarchical 'power culture' is becoming increasingly important as chambers become larger, the decisions become more complex and the market variables demand rapid reaction. If introduced, a chambers would need to adjust its structure to control the hierarchical power this would create, because in the wrong hands this could lead to internal conflict and frustrate decision-making. However, this is mitigated to some extent in a chambers culture

---

5   C Handy, *Understanding Organisations*, 4th Edition, Penguin, 1997.

because leadership, even in a 'power culture', can only be achieved through influence. The argument exists for a modern chambers model to strive for a blend of both cultures to drive its strategy successfully.

Therefore, the key cultural challenge for all chambers will be the cultural mismatches that will occur when a chambers addresses or changes its strategy. Understanding the cultural characteristics of a chambers will be increasingly important as the cultural mix that we discussed above becomes disrupted. The way things had been done previously in chambers may need to change to reflect a new strategy, and understanding the chambers' cultural characteristics will help to define the kind of strategy that can be successfully adopted. All of this requires buy-in, behavioural change and an understanding of the aims and objectives.

It should be noted that any cultural change in characteristics will have an impact on structure. So if you introduce the culture blend discussed above, your structure may need to change to reflect this.

3.2   Leadership

Leadership in chambers, even in a mix of 'person and power cultures', is about influencing members to come to a consensus in the decision-making. This in turn provides the commitment to delivering strategic aims.

Whether the leadership is coming from the management board, CEO or senior clerk, the challenge is that they are not the boss and do not have the ultimate authority over members. Leadership in a chambers structure is about having the skills to influence decision-making in a non-hierarchical style.

The peer group or team group style of leadership is an effective way to influence members of chambers. However, the key to this working successfully is having peer leaders or team leaders who possess the right characteristics to guide and facilitate these groups. These leaders need to understand and be aware of what is important to the people around them, have the trust and respect of those people, and the competence of leadership and the right skills. If you have people leading teams, groups or committees in chambers without these characteristics and skills, this will challenge your ability to reach the consensus needed to deliver strategy, and even if members and staff begin following they will soon find reasons, whether consciously or unconsciously, to drift, lose interest and eventually stop.

These influencing skills give the necessary alignment to achieve the buy-in and cooperation needed to drive strategy.

4.   Setting the competitive context and the pressure for change

In a rapidly changing legal landscape, gaining an understanding of how the future legal environment will look, as well as the impact of any competitive pressures in that environment, is integral to any strategic planning to ensure chambers is a sustainable business in the future. Even though adding this future environmental imaging to what has already been gained from historical data might increase the uncertainty, it does not remove the importance of analysing which factors could potentially drive change and how any change would impact on chambers operationally, tactically and strategically. Ignoring what is happening around you as a chambers and how it could impact on your business now and in the future is an unnecessary risk that can increase the potential for failure.

I have identified two forms of analysis that when used together will help to gain the insights needed and facilitate better strategic planning. There are others, but these are the key ones.

4.1 The macro environmental view

To analyse what the future competitive environment will look like for a chambers, it is necessary to identify the environmental factors that may influence the legal market and how those influences will impact on chambers. These influences can be best identified in six main types: political; economic; social; technological; environmental; and legal. These forces are linked, and change in one area drives change in another. Political agendas are driven by pressure from social issues, economic policy is affected by political strategies, and legislative changes are made to support these policies and drive change in the environment. The key questions you are asking in this analysis are: what environmental factors will affect growth of the legal environment? And what is the likely cumulative effect of all the things that affect growth?

A brief example of the sort of influences we are looking for and their long-term impact are the Legal Services Act 2007 and the 2008 financial crisis. Whilst these two key events happened some time ago and triggered significant change in the legal sector, the impact on most chambers has only really been felt over the last four years or so. A key impact of the financial crisis was to create downward pressure on professional fees as the balance of power between law firms and their clients altered, and the Legal Services Act 2007 was a driver for change by allowing non-lawyers to enter the legal market by owning and investing in law firms. These are two examples of the pressures and influences having an impact on growth of the legal environment that are now being felt by chambers, and whilst the financial crisis was arguably unforeseeable and therefore more difficult to plan for, the Legal Services Act and its impact were foreseeable.

Some current macro-environmental issues include technology, social attitudes to work, and diversity. Recently, artificial intelligence has been gathering momentum and we are starting to see this technological influence drive change in the way law firms do business. This, together with a social shift in the attitudes to work and leisure and diversity, is driving change in the working environment and having an impact on the law firm structure and chambers structure. Chambers should already be planning for the impact of these changes by analysing how these and other macro-environmental changes will shape the legal environment now and in the future. A chambers that does this effectively will be equipped to meet the challenges and exploit the opportunities that the new environment offers.

4.2 Competitive analysis

An assessment of the competitive environment overlaps with the longer-term macro analysis. However, it is easier for chambers to relate to because the time focus is more immediate and relevant. This type of analysis looks at the way existing competitors, new entrants, substituted pressures, client power and cost pressure impact on a chambers and its competitive position in the legal environment. Professor Michael Porter of Harvard Business School identified a framework known as the "five forces model" to explore these pressures. It should be noted that this analysis is highly relevant but does have its limitations. A much fuller analysis than is permitted in this chapter should feature the influence that 'globalisation', 'deregulation' and 'digitalisation' have on the five forces.

(a)   *Existing competitors*

In recent years the Bar has seen an increasing amount of strategic consolidation of chambers, movement of barristers between chambers, and in some situations the failure and dissolution of some sets. With competitive forces driving improved efficiencies, increased levels of specialism and organisational change, there is no suggestion that this trend is likely to end any time soon.

Any future analysis for chambers should involve scenario planning using existing competitors. This involves making assumptions about key competitors and then applying a probability to each scenario. By evaluating these potential influences using competitor scenarios, it should be possible to determine how quickly chambers could realign its structure, resources and strategy to respond if those probabilities became a reality.

The accurate selection and analysis of probable outcomes and their drivers enhances the ability of chambers to prepare for the future.

(b)   *New entrants*

The legal services environment has seen the competitive forces in the United Kingdom increase as non-lawyer entities react to client demand for efficiencies and improved levels of service through different structures.

The 2007 Legal Services Act gave a legal platform for non-lawyers to own and invest in law firms and finally enter the legal market. Over the last five years, after alternative business structures became possible in 2012 under the 2007 act, a significant number of new entrants, which include the 'Big Four' accountancy firms, have been developing their legal capability. Liberalising the market has also enabled new entrants, which include hedge funds and other investment vehicles, to acquire law firms.

All of this has been foreseeable for a number of years and for those chambers that have developed a strategy to address these changes, they should be able to mitigate the risks and benefit from the opportunities.

(c)   *Substitute pressures*

Alternative legal service providers are having an impact on process-driven legal services in areas such as disclosure, where they are able to provide improved efficiencies and services levels at a lower cost. Having gained access to this market, it is anticipated that there will be a push for more complex higher-value opportunities, such as providing draft contracts for financial services products or other high-value transactions, which will challenge the law firms.

All of this competitive pressure will be felt by chambers as law firms remodel to retain profit from pressurised revenue streams. Where the pressure from clients is for quicker and cheaper delivery of legal services, this might drive greater collaboration between law firms and alternative service providers. What chambers should be focused on is how in turn this would impact on them.

(d)   *Client power*

Client power has never been higher and all the signs suggest that this trend will continue for some time to come. The supply of legal services already significantly outstrips demand, and having a strategy to address client demands has never been more important with the balance of power firmly in favour of the consumer.

The Bar is a referral profession and therefore all the pressures felt by law firms in the business and legal environment are inevitably having an impact on chambers as these pressures are passed down the line.

The increasing demand from clients is for cost efficiencies and increased value in the delivery of service. This is driving change as clients look for the most cost-effective, high-quality, flexible options.

One thing seems certain, these changes are set to continue and a strategy to manage the threats and take advantage of the opportunities is essential for all chambers.

(e)   *Cost pressure*

The operating model for chambers supports a low-cost base, which is a significant advantage in a legal market where pressures on work streams exist. Innovative strategic thinking around the chambers structure allows for competitive advantage strategies in the form of 'cost leadership'.

5.   Conclusion and call to action

There is no doubt that planning a strategy in a fast-changing environment has its challenges, and the temptation to do nothing when the complexity of the current legal environment reduces predictability is in most cases the default option. Some chambers also feel they do not have the expertise or resources to undertake the strategic management process.

Hopefully this chapter has given some guidance about strategy and why it is important to have one. As you will have seen, you do not have to make the process excessively complex; it is about reflection, analysis, decision-making and action. Work out who you are and what you want to be, and measure this against your capabilities and skills. Work out your cultural characteristics and, most importantly, the ambitions of members and staff. Create a culture of leadership through influence, and work in collaboration with any professional managers. Finally, look ahead to see what is coming and assess how it will shape the future legal environment, as well as your competitive position within that environment. If you do this, you should be able to identify a vision statement of aims for chambers which matches the ambitions of members and staff, and a strategic plan of actions over a set time period to achieve this.

As in any professional services business, those chambers that best respond to the changing needs of clients and organise themselves to adapt to the environment around them will set the template for success. Not having a strategy will leave you drifting rudderless in turbulent waters.

Be the chambers that understands what is going on and makes things happen, not the chambers that looks on wondering what just happened!

Barristers' finance

Howard Sears
Price Bailey LLP

1.   Introduction

There are over 15,000 barristers practising in the United Kingdom who, alongside solicitors, are two of the main categories of lawyer in England and Wales. Barristers have traditionally had the role of handling cases in court, representing both defence and prosecution, while the solicitor's role has been the engagement of the client, investigating and gathering the evidence for the barrister.

Due to recent legislation, these traditional roles have now eroded, therefore meaning we now have solicitor advocates who can appear in court. The barrister can now take instructions directly from the client, but only with a solicitor, who may undertake work that requires funds to be held on behalf of a client. Despite these deliberate changes, which were designed to create new ways of capturing clients and new methods for conducting work, in many fields of practice the original and traditional distinction is largely retained.

This chapter on finance is intended to inform the 'independent Bar' and its 'sets of chambers'; it does not assist solicitors, who are usually 'in business' as partners in a general practice partnership, working together and sharing profits.

Barristers do not ordinarily share profits; they are in self-employed practice, operating within the framework of a set of chambers. Usually under a tenancy agreement, they pay a certain amount per month for rent, a percentage of their incomes, or a combination of the two to their chambers, which subsequently provides accommodation and a clerking service, which in many cases will help to provide a function for the sourcing and booking of work.

The head of chambers – usually a Queen's Counsel – will be responsible for managing the chambers alongside an appointed executive board made up of other elected members of the set. In effect, the members of the same set share the costs of running the chambers, but crucially each barrister remains an independent practitioner and is not responsible for the other barristers' business, as partners. Members of the same set of chambers may appear on opposite sides in the same case, remaining independent practitioners, being solely responsible for the conduct of their own practice and keeping what they earn.

The vast majority of the barristers practising in the United Kingdom are carrying out their work as members of a set of chambers and are essentially self-employed. The remaining practising barristers work at the 'employed Bar' for the government, the Crown Prosecution Service or in house in the legal departments of major corporations.

The following chapter will focus on the self-employed barrister at the independent Bar and the ever-demanding complexity of running a set of chambers.

2. Chambers

For a set of chambers to compete at the highest level, it must consider running its finances like a business. As with many other sectors and industries, technology is reducing the traditional boundaries of where individuals need to be to carry out their work. This therefore allows more home working, wherever that may be in the United Kingdom or abroad, providing opportunities for generating revenue throughout the world. Alongside these changes and ever-increasing legislation, a chambers needs to be highly organised if it is to capitalise on global opportunities for members, by creating an environment with a high level of financial sophistication to enable it to properly invest in technology, marketing, premises, people and finance.

Overall, the head of chambers, alongside his appointed executive committee members, must position their finances at the heart of their practice. So where do we start?

2.1 Regulation

The Bar Council – or the General Council of the Bar, to give it its full title – is the Bar's representative body. The Bar Standards Board – or the BSB – is the Bar's regulatory body.

In January 2014 the BSB issued a new handbook or 'code of conduct'. This was a key move towards smarter regulation and the BSB specifically identified some key processes that it expects to be competently managed – one of which is financial management.

Section IV specifically concerns chambers and self-employed barristers. It provides for the circumstances in which they can accept instructions. This section also contains further rules governing insurance, the duties of barristers and heads of chambers to administer their practice efficiently, and the rules about fees. Therefore, a good working knowledge of the handbook is important for barristers, heads of chambers and their executive.

2.2 Business structure

With so much commentary in the sector on new and innovative business structures available, the key question is which is the right option to choose?

A chambers is effectively an association of regulated individuals in an expense sharing arrangement. The chosen structure contracts with the outside world for premises, people and suppliers. The costs of these expenses are recharged to the regulated barrister members, who in turn make payment (maybe by deduction) back to the chambers. The net effect for many chambers is that all the costs are recharged and the expense sharing arrangement makes no surplus or deficit. This would be fine if it was not for the issue of tax and the potential need to make a surplus to help fund growth and working capital.

Traditionally, the expense sharing arrangements were making surpluses: they had received the contribution from the barrister but had not yet expended it, or they had spent money on entertaining, which was not allowable for tax, or they had purchased capital equipment, which was allowable for tax over an extended period. The expense sharing arrangement then had surpluses which, because it was an informal arrangement, were not being charged to tax, which caused issues for HMRC.

By contrast, self-employed barristers would just offset their contribution against their fees earned and pay tax on the profit. A further issue with this for HMRC was that the expense was actually a contribution to a whole lot of expenditure paid by chambers which might have included non-allowable tax deductions.

2.3 Trade protection associations

So to solve the problem HMRC encouraged discussions with the BSB for chambers to set up their expense sharing arrangements as if they were a trade protection association (TPA). This does not mean to say that chambers is actually an association; it may be that it has an incorporated body running chambers and the TPA is just a tax wrapper for the chambers structure, which provides tax reliefs for membership organisations.

Once registered with HMRC as a TPA, chambers is subject to corporation tax on any surpluses it makes and is able to obtain tax relief on any losses it makes. The *quid pro quo* is that all barristers' contributions paid are treated as tax deductible in their own accounts, without the worry that the expense included any non-tax-deductible element. As a general rule, whatever legal structure a chambers has, it is taxed as a mutual body.

2.4 Trading style

The expense sharing arrangement was often an informal arrangement traditionally in the name of the head of chambers. However, in recent times chambers have become, more often that not, branded with a trade name and the informal arrangement has given way to a corporate structure, which in turn has helped to protect the name. As it is a mutual arrangement for sharing costs, the corporate entities are often unlimited liability companies or limited by guarantee.

The corporate structure protects the head of chambers from being responsible for the debts of the set and spreads the risk among the members, albeit that some traditional sets in the name of the individual head would have sought protection by a formal legal agreement between the members.

2.5 Regulation of alternative business structures

The Solicitor Regulation Authority (SRA) was the first regulator of alternative business structures (ABSs) when these became commonplace as law firms moved to introduce non-lawyers into equity or manager status and wanted the benefit personally of limited liability protection. It was therefore not a surprise to see the BSB gain parliamentary approval to enable it to regulate ABSs in 2014.

Since then barristers have had the opportunity to form BSB-regulated entities that compete directly with SRA-regulated entities, including the involvement of non-lawyer owners and managers.

It would be wrong to underestimate the shift in attitudes required for the Bar Council and BSB to reach this stage. As a regulator, the BSB has long been focused on maintaining high standards and, more relevantly to business structures, independence.

In 2014, when the BSB was finally given approval to regulate entities, it was expected to be an attractive route for individual barristers, not least because of the potential corporation tax versus income tax savings. However, while this could still be attractive in some circumstances – particularly to those barristers with large outstanding work in progress (WIP) and debtor balances – the introduction of the 7.5% dividend income tax rate in the Finance Act in 2016 has removed much of the tax incentive. There are other reasons why barristers might consider this route, with potential limitation of liability being an obvious one.

At the same time, the BSB was also authorised to regulate multi-person entities, if owned and managed by authorised legal professionals. This opened up the possibility of barristers taking back control of their work streams, by creating entities that employ solicitors. They would then have the ability to effectively see the case through from cradle to grave, under the supervision and regulation of a familiar regulator – the BSB. The impact of independence rules means that the take up is likely to be limited, at least initially, but it does allow for innovative new businesses with barristers at the helm.

2.6 Funding chambers

Having considered the various structuring options available for chambers, the next key issue to consider is: how does a chambers fund its working capital such that it can meet its debts when they fall due?

This is a very real issue and one where a number of chambers have struggled to pay bills – particularly in the recent recession as solicitors were finding themselves at the end of a long queue to be paid and chambers at the end of that!

We have touched on the fact that chambers in its very course of carrying on business can create surpluses. This can be inevitable as it bills barristers for costs incurred which it has not yet contracted for due to the timing of payments. Of course, this is not popular for barristers, who will be attracted to a set which provides the best facilities at the lowest possible contribution and not a set that charges to create a surplus. However unpopular it might be to create a surplus, chambers does need to meet its debts when they fall due. So, having surpluses is one way to create some additional funds which can act as working capital.

There are other options available, which some manage with an overdraft, which is a simple buffer when cash flow tightens due to growth, or as a tax bill is due, or when the quarterly VAT payment is due. Bank loans are often used to manage longer-term projects such as the purchase of capital equipment, office fit out or maybe in the investment into the initiation of a new office in the United Kingdom or overseas. For a capital project, some sets will raise a bill for contribution to barristers.

A real problem can occur when a chambers quickly grows in size, coinciding with a sharp increase in the time clients take to pay fee notes. Robust credit control procedures need to be instigated to keep this under control and it is not uncommon for this to be a major problem for some chambers.

With many different parts to take into account, the budgeting process for chambers needs to be sophisticated, realistic and scientifically put together. When considering the budgeting process, significant consideration should be given to a reserves policy and chambers' billing and fees.

2.7 Chambers' reserve policy

Barristers' chambers are made up of many intelligent, independent-minded individuals and, as would be expected, this can lead to differing opinions and tensions over the level of expenditure within a set and, more importantly, how this feeds through to the members in terms of contribution levels and the calculation.

Arguably, the most significant of these issues is how individual chambers deal with any surpluses or deficits during a given period. Good budgeting is key to ensuring that any surpluses or deficits are as low as possible; however, budgets are by their nature an estimate and there are inevitably variances – sometimes quite large ones – when unexpected costs have been incurred, or barristers' income levels are significantly different to expectations.

This means that chambers' management needs to consider how to deal with general surpluses and deficits arising from the normal course of events and separately consider those arising from large projects or unexpected events.

Many chambers have no agreed policy for dealing with either of these issues and deal with them in differing, *ad hoc* and sometimes inconsistent ways. However, where deficits or large projects (or unexpected costs) are concerned this can lead to major problems for chambers, both from a cash flow and harmony perspective.

It is key that a consistent policy document is debated and agreed upon by chambers and its members. This creates a consistency of approach and expectation, and reduces the opportunity for conflict or financial problems for chambers. This should also deal with principles such as who funds certain costs (eg, present or future members). One example is a major refurbishment, whereby a member one year from retirement may feel it is unfair to pay the same as a member with 10 years in which to benefit from such a refurbishment. These are emotive issues and should be considered within any policy.

When formulating a policy it is important to consider the impact on cash flow and the amount of 'capital' required by chambers in terms of fixed and working capital. This also requires a decision on how to fund it. Most well-run and respected chambers will (or should) have a good relationship with their bank and if they use consistent and clear policies, as advocated above, they will usually have access to the funding required, whichever policy they choose.

The aim therefore is to explore the use of a more formal, transparent model for calculating the reserves required and, if applicable, any amounts required to be refunded to members. The model for calculating chambers' reserves and the credit for the year (if applicable) could then be enshrined into the company constitution, and be more visible to members.

This exercise is all the more important when significant capital expenditure is envisaged or undertaken so that the significant impact this can have on chambers' finances and corporation tax liabilities is fully understood in advance.

In order to fully understand the various options open to chambers' management in terms of a reserves policy, it is best to consider the reserves policy and the separate recharging of any large capital projects separately, before considering the combined effect later in this chapter.

The basic premise of chambers' reserves is that a chamber with nil reserves has, at each year-end, only charged its members for the expenditure it has incurred. There is no excess capital held. If chambers holds reserves, then the level of reserves is effectively the amount charged to barristers in advance, whether to fund working capital or for other reasons. In practice, leaving or retiring members usually have no right to be repaid their proportion of any reserves.

2.8   Options

Broadly speaking, the options available are:

- A) the *ad hoc* approach;
- B) holding no working capital or reserves; or
- C) a set reserves figure.

(a)   The ad hoc *approach*

Advantages:

- management retain flexibility.

Disadvantages:

- lack of transparency;
- can cause a reluctance to ask for more if budget overspends occur;
- receipts and accommodation rates often based on budgeted forecast year-end results, not actual;
- time consuming around year-end; and
- potential lack of consistency.

(b)   *Holding no working capital or reserves*

Advantages:

- automatically calculated, based on final figures;
- zero reserves tied up;
- minimal (or zero) members capital tied up; and
- corporation tax savings maximised (no surplus profits).

Disadvantages:

- needs bank to fund day-to-day working capital; and
- members' security potentially required for overdraft.

(c)   *A set reserves figure*

This approach could set a total figure to be held in respect of working capital of, say, £200,000 or a set figure per member of, say, £10,000. Therefore, each member would have capital committed to fund chambers' working capital of £10,000. This would make it relatively easy to repay leaving members and charge new members on arrival.

For new members, centrally arranged bank funding may be available to pay this initial amount.

Advantages:
- easy to understand;
- automatically calculated, based on final figures; and
- allows leaving members to be repaid.

Disadvantages:
- if bank funding not available, new members may not want or be able to pay £10,000 up-front.

2.9 Preliminary conclusion

For the sake of transparency, and ignoring the impact of any significant capital spends for now, it would appear that options B) and C) offer significantly more transparency and accountability. Which method is used would potentially depend on whether a bank overdraft is available. If it is, then option B) would be easier and more simplistic to implement; if not, it may be a necessity to implement option C).

2.10 Options for dealing with significant capital spends

In the past, many chambers have funded major refurbishment projects by recharging members on a *per capita* basis. Therefore, if £500,000 was spent and there are 50 members, each member would be recharged £10,000, irrespective of seniority. The rationale being that junior members, who would pay less if the refurbishment were to be incorporated into the receipts charge, will in theory benefit as much, if not more, than the more senior members, so should share the cost equally. Chambers sometimes arrange a loan facility so that any member can repay their proportion over five years if they do not have access to the up-front capital. For simplicity, it will be assumed for the remainder of this chapter that all members pay up front in this scenario.

The disadvantage of this approach has been that while most of the capital spend does not attract corporation tax relief, the recharge to members does. Therefore, assuming a flat rate of corporation tax of 20%, this could cost chambers £100,000 in corporation tax. However, with a combined approach to the reserves policy, this can be mitigated, as explained later.

The options available in respect of the proposed refurbishment expenditure are believed to be:
- recharge members *per capita*;
- fund from receipts charge; or
- landlord fund and recharge via increased rent.

A combination of these approaches can also be adopted.

(a) Recharge members per capita

Advantages:
- simple to calculate and explain; and
- no effect on day-to-day cash flow.

Disadvantages:
- corporation tax charge is high; and
- members close to retirement may still begrudge paying circa £10,000.

The negative aspect of who pays for what could be mitigated by refunding any member leaving within, say, five years a *pro rata* amount of the cost. New joiners could also be charged *pro rata* if joining within the next five years.

(b) **Fund from receipts charge**
Advantages:
- covered by normal budgeting and accounting processes.

Disadvantages:
- considerable increase in receipts charge in year of project;
- high earners pay more than low earners;
- corporation tax charge still high; and
- refurbishment paid in year 1 so future members pay nothing towards the refurbishment, whereas retiring members pay in full.

The significant up-front hike could be mitigated by recharging over five years and taking out a bank loan to offset the cash flow impact.

(c) **Landlord fund and recharge via increased rent**
This would have no effect on the current balance sheet, but would lead to increased costs moving forward.
Advantages:
- removes need for chambers to fund project;
- all costs fully tax allowable for chambers; and
- paid for by members of chambers benefiting from use.

Disadvantages:
- unlikely to be a fast approval process within the Inn; and
- likely to be more expensive.

2.11 Banking

Having worked out a reserves policy, the banking arrangements for chambers can be considered. Most high street banks are keen to attract barristers as personal customers and chambers as business customers.

As in any sector, the key is always to meet with a bank as early as possible in the process of borrowing money. A business/strategic plan, alongside a detailed budget and cash flow forecast, will be the minimum requirements to ensure that the bank has the appetite to make the advance.

Chambers have traditionally funded their requirements through an overdraft facility to manage VAT, PAYE and quarterly rent payments due. However, a growing and developing chambers cannot rely on such a method if it wants to move the set forward. An expanding chambers will need loan capital to fund a growing debtor and WIP book, which sits alongside a large workforce which needs paying every month and cannot wait for the client to pay. Overdrafts work fine so long as they are used to smooth out the peaks and troughs, but banks do not like these to become hard-core borrowing.

It is unusual to ask barrister members for capital, but with the onset of new contemporary structures those forward-thinking chambers are making it work for them, just like a standard solicitors' practice. In solicitor law firms, and other professional practices, partners have provided capital personally in the form of a capital subscription loan to the partnerships. This is a loan direct to the partner personally, who is responsible for its repayment and the financing of the interest. The loan is invested into the practice and becomes capital for that partner who has it returned when he or she leaves. The loan can be interest only or capital repayment.

Many banks will earmark a facility for the members of a practice. The bank will take security by a letter of undertaking that confirms that the firm will pay back to the bank before it returns any sum to the barrister member. Due diligence on the member is done at a high level, making it an easy facility for the member to enter into.

2.12   Central fees account

A number of chambers have set up and run a bank account for collecting fees centrally. There are a number of benefits for chambers of doing this, with the key advantage being that chambers do not need to rely on the individual barristers to notify them of receipt.

When fee notes are sent out the bank details for the central fee account can be placed on the invoice. It also helps members to ensure that their VAT returns are correct, with the information coming straight from chambers on a timely basis.

However, these advantages come with a risk. The crucial issue when managing a central fee account is the risk that this account is not properly maintained and reconciled. With it being a transitory account it needs to be properly managed and controlled.

2.13   Accounting systems and procedures

(a)   *Practice management*

There are many different types of chambers management software available. Popular examples of these software packages are Lex and Meridian, which are key to how chambers administer the recording of members' work done and raising fees to, and collecting the money from, clients. By administering this centrally, for all the barristers, it allows chambers to obtain the economies of scale of only having one set of software costs.

Barristers generally bill on an hourly basis. These hours are recorded in the central software by the clerks and specialist fees clerks. These hours are then periodically billed to clients. The clerks or fees clerk will raise the fee note and send it to the client and record it as appropriate in the chambers' management software.

The fees clerk will then be responsible for liaising with the client (usually a solicitor) to obtain payment and recording the money as received. This allows the reports to be run detailing each barrister's receipt for a relevant period and the receipts contribution to be calculated.

(b) *Barristers' contribution (recharging) software*

As yet, none of the available practice management software packages has the facility to then calculate the level of contribution each barrister is required to make. Chambers have many ways of recording and calculating such contributions, including excel spreadsheets. However, many chambers now use separate, access-based software packages to calculate the amount of accommodation and receipts charges due to members and administer the member specific recharges. Popular examples are Bar Stat and Chamber Pot. These software packages will then produce the periodic invoice to members showing a detailed breakdown of what they are being recharged for.

(c) *Accounting software*

Most chambers then use a traditional off-the-shelf accounting package to record all of their income and expenses. This is usually administered by an accountant, finance manager, bookkeeper or combination thereof.

In many cases the recharging software, such as Bar Stat, will automatically pull in data from Sage in order to calculate recharges and will also then transfer the data relating to fees raised to members back into Sage. This saves a significant amount of administration time, compared to the manual recharging methods available.

(d) *Cloud accounting*

With the pace of technology there is now a range of accounting system solutions available to enhance and streamline bookkeeping and processing requirements. Over the past 18 months, the accounting profession has seen one of the biggest changes in management information systems since the introduction of spreadsheets. This has arisen as a result of ongoing technological advances across the globe and the increased demand for real time data. The use of online accounting software has increased exponentially and the benefits of using online solutions are numerous.

2.14 **Managing risk through internal control**

Chambers can be measured in different ways. One way is to view it as a simple expense sharing arrangement. What could go wrong? Expenses of £3 million recharged back to the members at £3 million. Of course this is not the whole story because chambers is administrating all the fees for all the members. With expenses of £3 million, turnover for the whole set might be £9 million and with VAT that is over £11 million of cash income to be managed. Of course each set of chambers is different and when looked at as one entity the turnover of some sets might be heading over £50 million.

A chambers is like any other corporate structure and needs to ensure that proper controls are implemented by the executive committee.

2.15   **Objectives of internal control**
Internal control should have the following objectives.

(a)   ***Efficient conduct of business***
Controls should be in place to ensure that processes flow smoothly and operations are free from disruptions. This mitigates against the risk of inefficiencies and threats to the value in the organisation.

(b)   ***Safeguarding assets***
Controls should be in place to ensure that assets are deployed for their proper purposes and are not vulnerable to misuse or theft. A comprehensive approach to this objective should consider all assets, including both tangible and intangible assets.

(c)   ***Preventing and detecting fraud and other unlawful acts***
Even small businesses with simple organisational structures may fall victim to these violations, but as organisations increase in size and complexity, the nature of fraudulent practices becomes more diverse and controls must be capable of addressing them.

(d)   ***Completeness and accuracy of financial records***
An organisation cannot produce accurate financial statements if its financial records are unreliable. Systems should be capable of recording transactions so that the nature of business transacted is properly reflected in the financial accounts.

(e)   ***Timely preparation of financial statements***
Organisations should be able to fulfil their legal obligations to submit their accounts accurately and on time. They also have a duty to their shareholders to produce meaningful statements; internal controls may also be applied to management accounting processes, which are necessary for effective strategic planning, decision taking and monitoring of organisational performance.

2.16   **Responsibilities for internal control**
In many smaller, unincorporated chambers, the responsibility for internal controls often lies with the head of chambers. In most cases, the head is fully engaged in chambers itself and it is usually within the capability of the head to remain fully aware of transactions and the overall state of the business.

As chambers grow, the need for internal controls increases, as the degree of specialisation increases and it becomes impossible to remain fully aware of what is going on in every part of the business.

In a limited company such as a set of chambers, the executive board of directors is responsible for ensuring that appropriate internal controls are in place. The board's accountability is to the barrister members, as the directors act as their agents. In turn, the directors may consider it prudent to establish a dedicated internal control function. The point at which this decision is taken will depend on the extent to which the benefits of function will outweigh the costs.

The directors must pay due attention to the control environment. If internal controls are to be effective, it is necessary to create an appropriate culture and embed a commitment to robust controls throughout the organisation.

2.17 Taxation

Whatever the expense sharing structure a chambers decides to adopt, if it has been registered as a TPA, then it will be subject to corporation tax. Corporation tax will be charged at 19% (falling to 17% by 2020/21) on the taxable profits of the structure.

Corporation tax is self-assessed and an annual corporation tax return must be completed and filed with HMRC. The basis of assessment for the taxable profits is the tax adjusted trading profits for the chargeable accounting period (ie, no more than 12 months) on accounts prepared under generally accepted accounting principles (GAAP).

The reason that accounts need to be adjusted for tax purposes is because corporation tax does not use exactly the same rules as financial accounting under GAAP. The taxable profit is based on the tax rules. For example, there are some costs that are legitimate from an accounting point of view but are not allowable as deductions in arriving at the profit figure for tax purposes.

The objective of adjusting the financial accounts is to make sure that:
- the only income that is credited is trading income; and
- the only expenditure deducted is allowable trading income.

An adjusted profit computation is produced, which in effect cancels out income and expenditure that is not relevant for tax purposes.

(a) *Adjusting income*

The following income is not assessable as trading income:
- non-trading interest receivable;
- rent receivable;
- gains on the disposal of fixed assets; and
- dividends received.

Non-trading interest and rent received will reappear and be included in the taxable total profits in the computation under investment income. Gains on the disposal of fixed assets could result in chargeable gains.

(b) *Adjusting expenditure*

Only expenditure which is non-allowable will need to be added back to the financial profits. The general rule for expenditure to be allowable is that it must be:
- revenue rather than capital in nature; and
- wholly and exclusively for the purpose of the trade.

The following are examples of expenditure that is not allowable:
- capital expenditure;
- depreciation and amortisation;

- entertaining;
- gifts;
- fines; and
- certain legal expenses.

Specific allowable expenditure includes capital allowances. When assets are purchased for the business – such as office equipment and furniture etc – capital allowances are available. As with expenses, these are deducted from income to calculate the taxable profit.

(c) Annual Investment Allowance

The Annual Investment Allowance (AIA) gives a 100% write off on most types of expenditure, but not cars up to a value of £200,000 per annum. Any costs in excess of the AIA will attract an annual ongoing allowance of 8% or 18% depending on the type of asset.

(d) Dealing with losses

If once the profits have been adjusted and any capital allowances deducted the result is a minus figure, a trading loss will have arisen. As a result:
- the trading assessment for tax will be nil in that year; and
- the negative figure will form the trading loss that will be able to be relieved against future profits or carried back to the previous chargeable accounting period.

2.18 VAT

A set of chambers that is a TPA has an obligation to register for VAT. The following rules apply:
- VAT will be charged on all supplies, which will include contributions levied on members;
- VAT incurred on expenditure will be recoverable under normal rules; and
- completion of a VAT return in the name of chambers will be done quarterly.

The barristers registered for VAT will be able to recover the VAT charged on their contributions by chambers. Barristers that are not registered for VAT will not be able to recover VAT charged. VAT-registered barristers are entitled to claim VAT inputs in relation to elements of chambers' expenses.

Sets of chambers are free to adopt one of the following methods that best works for them. Once they have adopted a system, they should maintain the same system. Broadly speaking, HMRC needs to be comfortable that the correct VAT input has been claimed and records need to be maintained to ensure this is the case.

(a) Method 1

The nominated member to whom the invoice is addressed treats the full amount of VAT as input tax. He accounts for the output tax on the shares recharged to members. Members who are VAT registered claim it back as input tax.

(b)   *Method 2*

The nominated member to whom the invoice is addressed does not charge VAT to the other members of the chambers. Instead the input tax is apportioned so that the VAT-registered members can claim it back on the basis of their own contributions.

(c)   *Method 3*

The nominated member to whom the invoice has been addressed deducts the whole amount of the input tax and pays an equal amount of money into the common fund. This method may only be used when all the members of chambers are registered for VAT.

2.19   Employment and pensions

Barristers are self-employed at the independent Bar and do not receive a salary; however, a set of chambers is no different from any other employer and there are key things that it will need to do when it comes to having employees.

(a)   *Financial issues*

The following financial rules apply:

- chambers will need to register as an employer with HMRC up to four weeks before it pays its first new employee;
- it will need to either operate a payroll or employ an accountant or bookkeeper to do it on its behalf;
- it will need to ensure that it pays at least the National Minimum Wage (NMW) amount (currently £7.05 for employees 21 and over); and
- it will need employer's liability insurance.

(b)   *Legal issues*

The following legal rules apply:

- Chambers as employer will need to be aware of some of the basic employment rights which apply from day one of employment. These include having a right to:
    - an itemised payslip;
    - holiday;
    - NMW;
    - statutory sick pay;
    - health and safety protection;
    - time off for children/dependants; and
    - protection against discrimination.
- Before offering a job, chambers must ensure it has completed the following basic checks:
    - do they have the right to work in the United Kingdom?
    - references; and
    - criminal record checks where necessary (now called DBS checks).
- Chambers must keep records on the following:
    - rates of pay;
    - payroll (ie, tax and National Insurance);

- sickness absence; and
- accidents and injuries.
- Chambers must be aware of the following data protection issues:
  - personal info must be relevant, adequate and not excessive; and
  - workers can see their records on request.
- By law, chambers must have in place the following:
  - discipline and grievance procedures;
  - health and safety measures if employing more than five employees; and
  - a written statement of particulars – basic terms of employment (within two months of the employee commencing employment).

(c)   ***HR issues***

It is likely that at some stage chambers will encounter challenges with managing the team. Creating policies to deal with the following issues can really help:

- performance;
- absence;
- behaviour and conduct (eg, use of computer systems and social media); and
- conflict.

Finding the right candidate is absolutely essential. Taking time to consider exactly what role chambers wants an employee to undertake and what type of candidate it is looking for is key. Chambers should not use general job descriptions or job adverts – these should be made specific to chambers' business and needs, and in line with its strategic planning.

HR initiatives demonstrate their value when they enhance or support the achievement of business goals and help to eliminate or reduce risk and cost. The Oxford Economics Workforce 2020 research cites inabilities to retain employees, lack of adequate leadership, skills shortages, internal resources (eg, competitive pay) and technology as major obstacles to meeting future workplace goals. 2016 saw the continued uptake of companies turning to M&A and corporate venturing to achieve growth and harness technology.

As UK productivity continues to fall in the service sector – with some arguing that much of this lies at the door of professional services – businesses are searching for alternative delivery models to meet client expectations, differentiate themselves from the competition and ensure they are well positioned to respond to increasing environmental and regulatory changes and requirements.

Against this backdrop, stress accounted for 37% of work-related ill health cases in the United Kingdom in 2015/16, with the main factors being workplace pressure, tight deadlines, too much responsibility and lack of managerial support. 1.7 million small business owners – the engine room of the UK economy – say they are unhappy with their work–life balance and research suggests they are working 13 hours per week more than the average UK employee.

The need, therefore, for effective employee engagement is becoming increasingly important in this rapidly changing world of work that is challenging traditional concepts of command and control leadership. Winning hearts and minds is the key to attracting and retaining the talent required to build and sustain the business for the long term. Now more than ever, the appropriate identification, prioritisation and implementation of HR/people initiatives are becoming critical to business success.

2.20 Pupillage

A pupillage is the final vocational stage of training for those wishing to become practising barristers. The financial position of pupils varies enormously. Some barristers will earn £12,000 (the Bar Council minimum) for a 12-month pupillage in a criminal set; while a pupillage in a top commercial set could be paid up to £65,000. The Bar Council has decreed that all pupils must be paid £1,000 per month, which must be made up of a minimum of £6,000 in the first six months and guaranteed earnings of £6,000 in the second six.

It is usual practice for chambers to allow pupils to retain all second six earnings in excess of this amount, although these can be subject to deductions for clerking, chambers expenses and other sums.

While pupils are allowed to supplement their incomes by undertaking part-time work outside of their pupillages with the permission of the head of chambers, the Bar Council requires pupils to apply themselves full time. The EU Working Time Directive applies to pupillages. A barrister commencing his practice at the beginning of the second six months of pupillage is accepted by HMRC.

Pupillage awards from the Inns are treated as scholarships and are totally exempt from income tax. Pupillage awards received from chambers are not regarded as scholarships and are fully taxable. There is, however, an exception to this rule: if the awards from chambers are received within the first six months of pupillage, they are normally exempt. This is why, in-practice awards, if any, from chambers are more generally paid within the first six months of pupillage than the second six.

3. Barristers

3.1 Practice structure for the individual barrister

Most barristers are self-employed and have the status of a sole trader business. This is the simplest form of business structure as it can be established without legal formality. The business of a sole trader is not distinguished from the proprietor's personal affairs. As such, if the business incurs debts which are unpaid, creditors can seek repayment from the sole trader personally.

Until recent changes in legislation driven by the Clementi review and the Legal Services Act 2007 that followed, the BSB was only authorised to regulate sole traders and their chambers.

3.2 Income tax

The following income tax rules apply to barristers:
- The majority of barristers are self-employed for tax purposes, running their business in their own name. Income tax is charged on the taxable profits for the business in each tax year and is based on the tax rules which are included in the Income Tax (Trading and Other Income) Act 2005.

- An annual self-assessment tax return will need to be prepared and filed by the barrister, which will report all of his income and capital gains in each fiscal year to 5 April.
- The filing deadline for the tax return is 31 January following the end of the tax year.
- The tax due will be calculated taking into account all of the barrister's income from all sources. This will include the earned income as a self-employed barrister together with any other income, including unearned income from investments and property income.
- In the first year tax will be payable on 31 January following 5 April.
- In subsequent years tax will be due in two instalments known as payments on account (POA) on 31 January and 31 July. The POA is calculated based on the earnings of the previous year's return. Any amount underpaid if earnings have increased will be collected on the following 31 January. If income has gone down, then an application can be made to reduce the POA.
- Income tax will be calculated at the marginal rate of tax based on the rates etc in that year.
- There is an automatic penalty for late filing of a return of £100. This will always be due if a return is filed late, even if there is no tax due.

3.3 Calculation of taxable profits

The basic rules are that the profits of a trade must be calculated in accordance with GAAP, subject to any adjustment required or authorised by law in calculating profits for income tax or corporation tax purposes.

3.4 Basis of computation of trading profits of barristers and advocates

(a) Commencement of practice

A 'barrister' is defined as a person who is qualified, or who has a right, to plead at the bar in a court of law. A newly qualified barrister, unless exempted by his Inn of Court, must complete a year's practical training (the pupillage period), during the first six months of which he cannot accept instructions or conduct any part of a case himself. The profession of barrister, therefore, cannot in any event commence before the end of the first six months of pupillage. While the question of when the profession commences is therefore one of fact, the most likely date of commencement is that on which the barrister is in a position to accept briefs and has instructed the clerk to obtain such briefs.

Any fees received prior to the commencement of the practice (eg, fees from the writing of articles etc) should be assessed as miscellaneous income (under Part 5 Chapter 8) of the Income Tax (Trading and Other Income) Act 2005.

(b) Barristers and advocates in early years of practice

Under Section 160 of the Income Tax (Trading and Other Income) Act 2005, barristers and advocates are specifically permitted to use an alternative to GAAP in their early years of practice if they were using that alternative in the tax year 2012/13.

(c)   **Alternative basis**

Barristers and advocates are regarded as commencing in practice when they first hold themselves out as available for fee-earning work.

Barristers or advocates in practice for a period of not more than seven years after commencement of practice may compute their profits:

- on a cash basis (ie, receipts are recognised as income of the period in which they are received and expenses as outgoings of the period in which they are paid. All debtors, creditors, stock and WIP are excluded); or
- by reference to fees earned whose amount has been agreed or in respect of which a fee note has been delivered.

Once a particular basis has been adopted, it must be applied consistently. The alternative basis described above ceases to apply if for any period the barrister or advocate prepares his trading profits under GAAP. In that event all future periods of account must be prepared on a GAAP basis.

A barrister or advocate who ceases to practise for a period and then recommences cannot adopt the alternative basis for the subsequent period if, as a question of fact, this is more than seven years after he first commenced practice or the trading profits have previously been prepared under GAAP.

Barristers currently using the alternative basis for the tax year 2012/13 will be able to continue to do so until the period of account ending not more than seven years after commencement of practice.

For the tax year 2013/14, newly qualified barristers will not be able to use the alternative basis of calculating their profits, but may be eligible to use the new cash basis.

(d)   **Cash basis: eligibility**

Under Sections 31A–31D and 148K of the Income Tax (Trading and Other Income) Act 2005, a person may elect for his profits or losses to be calculated on the cash basis instead of in accordance with GAAP for a tax year if he meets all the conditions below:

- the total cash basis receipts for all trades carried on by the person in a tax year do not exceed the relevant maximum amount;
- where the person is either an individual who controls a partnership or a partnership controlled by an individual or partnership in a tax year does not exceed the relevant maximum amount and the individual or partnership uses the cash basis for all those trades; and
- the person is not excluded from using the cash basis.

If a person elects to use the cash basis for a tax year, he must use the cash basis for each trade he carries out during that tax year.

Cash basis receipts are those received during the basis period for the tax year and which would be brought into account in calculating the profits of the trade for that tax year on the cash basis. The cash basis is available for unincorporated businesses only; companies and limited liability partnerships cannot use it.

(e)   *Calculating income under GAAP*

The following rules apply when calculating income under GAAP:

- The profits for a self-employed individual are based on when the income has been earned and not when the cash is received. Income needs to be calculated in accordance with GAAP.
- Any net increase/decrease in a barrister's WIP at the year-end needs to be added to the fees raised in the period of account.
- In calculating the value of WIP the barrister needs to include an estimate of how much the fee is likely to be based on the work completed at the year-end. For completed work at the year-end the WIP is the value of the bill raised in the following accounting period.
- Where conditional fee agreements are in place, no amount needs to be brought in until the contingent event has happened.
- Legal aid work should be recognised as the work is completed in the same way and not when paid by the Legal Services Commission.
- For any fees that have been raised but are not or unlikely to be paid, tax relief may be obtained and they can be included as bad debts.
- At the end of the seventh year of cash accounting the barrister will need to calculate the value of his WIP and the amount of debtors (fees unpaid). These amounts are included. This amount is known as adjusted income and brought into tax with an allowance that the amount due can be paid over 10 years.

(f)   *Calculating expenditure under GAAP*

The following rules apply when calculating expenditure under GAAP:

- Deductible business expenditure is that which has been incurred in the year, which may include expenses not yet paid.
- Business expenditure incurred wholly and exclusively for business purposes will be categorised into revenue and capital nature.
- Capital expenditure will be for the cost of assets that will have a useful economic life of more than 12 months. This would include such items as furniture and equipment and computer technology.
- Revenue expenditure will be of a consumable nature for expenses incurred to run the practice in each year.
- The main revenue expenditure will be the contribution to chambers, professional indemnity insurance, library and subscriptions, hotels and travelling, staff costs, rent, bank charges and telecoms.

(g)   *Expenditure on clothing*

Barristers should allow a deduction in computing profits for the cost of replacing gowns and wigs and frock coats worn by Queen's Counsel. These are classed as allowable expenses.

Barristers should not allow a deduction for expenditure on 'normal clothes' – for example, black coats and pinstripe trousers worn by male barristers or black dresses and suits worn by female barristers. These are classed as non-allowable expenses.[1]

---

1   See *Mallalieu v Dummond* (1983) 57 TC 330.

(h) **Business records**

HMRC requires books of account and business records be retained for up to five years following the end of the year of assessment. The BSB Handbook requires the barrister to keep his individual practice efficient and properly administered, and proper records should be kept.

3.5   VAT

Both chambers and barristers are impacted by the rules on VAT. The rules are complex, and contained within this section is information on the VAT invoicing rules and place of supply rules in general, applicable to barristers.

(a) **What is the tax point of a barrister's services?**

Normally the actual tax point for the provision of services is the invoice date. However, barristers benefit from special tax point rules for VAT purposes. Services supplied by a barrister shall be treated as taking place at whichever is the earliest of the following times:
- when the fee in respect of those services is received by the barrister or advocate;
- when the barrister or advocate issues a VAT invoice in respect of them; or
- the day on which the barrister or advocate ceases to practise as such.

This means that, in general, a barrister will only need to account for the output tax in relation to a supply in the VAT period in which he receives payment. The special tax point rules only affect the tax point of supplies made by the barrister. Input tax can be recovered in reference to the date on the purchase invoice rather than when the invoice amount is paid.

(b) **How does the cash accounting scheme work?**

While the special tax point for barristers means that a tax point is not generated on the completion of the barrister's services, a tax point is created on the date that a VAT invoice is raised in respect of the fees. Thus, as soon as a VAT invoice is created rather than a fee report, the VAT will become due in the quarter in which the invoice was raised, irrespective of payment.

Cash accounting is an alternative method of accounting for VAT. The usual tax point rules are dispensed with and instead:
- output VAT on supplies a business makes is accounted for on the VAT return in the period in which payment is received from the customer; and
- input VAT on supplies a business purchases may only be recovered on the VAT return in the period in which it makes the payment to its supplier.

The raising of a VAT invoice for cash-accounting purposes therefore has no effect on the tax point of the supply. The major advantage of the cash accounting scheme is improved cash flow and automatic bad debt relief. To be eligible to use this scheme the expected value of taxable supplies (excluding VAT) in the next 12 months must not exceed £1,350,000. After having joined the scheme, if the value of a business's taxable supplies in the previous 12 months exceeds £1,600,000, it will be required to leave the scheme.

The special tax point rules for barristers work in much the same way but the main differences are as follows:

- there is no upper turnover threshold in relation to using the barristers' special tax point;
- the raising of a VAT invoice within the barristers' special rules does create a tax point; and
- barristers can recover input tax as and when an invoice is received. Under cash accounting, input tax can only be recovered once the purchase payment has been made.

Cash accounting may be worth considering for those barristers whose turnover is well under the cash accounting upper threshold. If a barrister joins the cash accounting scheme, he must use the scheme for the whole of his business. On leaving the cash accounting scheme, the barrister will need to account for any undeclared VAT even if he has received payment from the customer. There may also be cases where the business has not paid its suppliers and has not yet claimed the input tax. On leaving the cash accounting scheme, a business is entitled to claim this input tax subject to the normal VAT rules.

This chapter represents the views of the author and readers should not rely on the content for legal or financial advice.

Practice management and business development

Paul Martenstyn
Alex Taylor
Fountain Court Chambers – London & Singapore

1. Introduction

We operate in a highly competitive market. Over the past decade or so, practice management and business development activities have become increasingly important for barristers and their chambers. In this chapter we set out some tips and guidance which have helped us to achieve success – both for individual members and chambers as a whole. Of course, clear, well-directed and strong management has also played a role in achieving this success, but effective practice management and business development initiatives have had a direct benefit too and should not be underestimated.

Why practice management? Everybody needs a plan and goals. It is no longer possible for barristers to expect the work they desire to come flooding into them. Barristers should take responsibility for their practice. Clerking teams have an extraordinary amount of combined knowledge and relationships among them and can offer vital assistance. Well-motivated and directed teams will be able to deploy this knowledge and effect the right introductions for members to lead them along their so-desired career paths. Of course, fellow members of chambers can also assist in making introductions and providing guidance to members, particularly those who might be more junior.

Business development has also come to the fore. This will be influenced by the outcome of individual practice review meetings. The concept is to create openings to increase work opportunities with new clients and allow barristers to break into new areas of work. One section of our chapter will cover relationships. As a referral profession, relationships are crucial to barristers, both in generating new ones and – equally as important – in maintaining existing ones. We shall also cover resourcing of business development teams. However, the clerks are the people who have the day-to-day contact with members and clients of chambers, and they are consequently the best equipped to maintain and develop these relationships.

None of this is radical, but in a fast-changing and competitive arena, the basic and simple things always need to be done well.

As sets of chambers become brand names, one emerging tension is the balance between the individual barristers and the collective. For example, a set might have a reputation for acting for banks and be viewed in the market as such. How does this sit with other barristers in the same chambers who act against banks? Furthermore, what might be the view of the banks knowing that members of their perceived set are on their opposing side in disputes? This must be carefully managed to ensure that the relationships are not jeopardised from all sides, and the clerking team can cover this in practice management meetings.

2. Practice management

2.1 What is 'practice management'?

The long-established (and in the eyes of some, but not the author, antiquated) practice of clerking barristers is genuinely unique. Although it has no equivalent among the other professions with which barristers interact, it is a practice that is here to stay and a potent reminder of the fundamentally human nature of the closely held relationship between a clerk and his barrister. Daily, this relationship involves regular communication, managing expectations and (when needed) providing reassurance. A clerk should always aim to think ahead of his barrister, and always have a plan B.

In any chambers, each barrister's individual practice is an individual 'business', albeit a business that exists within the overarching chambers' ecosystem, which of course includes other individual barristers' own businesses. A logical, realistic, bespoke and agreed strategy is required to allow each of these individual businesses to operate as efficiently as possible. This is where the concept of 'practice management' comes into play.

2.2 Practice management systems

Although daily communication is essential, at the point of delivery, an effective practice management system involves the members of the practice management team assigned to any individual barrister sitting down regularly in person with that barrister to discuss the current state of, and the outlook for, his practice. It is critically important for those managing members' practices to make every reasonable effort to understand the member's own perceptions of his individual practices as well as his individual goals and ambitions. The practice management meeting is at the heart of any effective practice management system.

The human element of the clerk/barrister relationship works best when both stakeholders are motivated to work together to achieve agreed objectives. However, that motivation is impossible to achieve in the absence of effective communication – an obvious yet crucial point which is often overlooked. To be effective, that communication must extend beyond a clerking team unilaterally attempting to understand a barrister's objectives and challenges. At its core, it must also include such fundamental matters as facilitating regular '360-degree' feedback and establishing a mutually agreed programme of regular meetings with the barrister. Any long-term strategy is unlikely to have realistic prospects of success without proper consideration of matters such as these.

There is of course a great deal more involved in setting up an effective practice management system if it is to work as intended. The team of individuals running and managing a set of chambers must be proactive and visible to barrister members on both institutional and individual levels. By way of background, the barristers' chambers business model is radically different to that of a law firm. Each barrister has his own unique business model and, as set out above, owns and operates his own individual business, which on one level 'competes' with the business of other barristers, whether inside or outside his chambers. Because each barrister member of a set of chambers is self-employed, albeit while working under the same roof, each individual's business model (and that of chambers as a whole) is completely different from that of a law firm and its constituent partners. While the partners in a law firm, in practice, are legitimately expected to adhere to a particular business strategy – working together as part of a partnership – the simple fact is that each individual barrister in any set of chambers is likely to have his own view on strategy, reflecting the differing nature of each barrister's practice. The chambers model must therefore cater for this fundamental difference. In practice, this means that the practice management model needs to allow for a considerable degree of flexibility in its conception and execution.

It is also fundamentally important to the implementation of any successful practice management system that the practice manager has given careful prior consideration to a set of clear objectives in advance of the practice review meeting. This is essential to identify a realistic and therefore achievable idea of what the barrister expects from this meeting. Setting realistic short- and long-term objectives builds trust and confidence between the barrister, who will hopefully directly benefit from those objectives, and the individual who administers the member's practice. Preparation in advance of any practice review meeting is therefore critically important. This includes having considered in advance of the meeting all the necessary information, such as:

- work enquiry statistics;
- work done figures (ie, billing);
- payments (ie, receipts) and aged debt figures, pegged to particular time periods (eg, quarterly, six-monthly, annual and yearly+); and
- all other relevant general marketing data.

On a practical level, a sample (or model) practice review meeting agenda might be as follows:

- General: the 'how are you getting on' or pastoral care element of the meeting;
- 'State of the nation': considering discussing the member's practice by reference to previously identified objectives and identifying at a high level the objectives for the practice as at the date of the meeting;
- Financials: work done, payments, aged debt, etc (see above);
- Identity of current client base;
- Marketing activities: current and proposed;
- Practice areas: review of current practice areas and consideration of any additional areas in which the member may be interested, by reference to areas in which chambers' general marketing infrastructure may be able to assist;
- Review of clerking services and feedback in both directions;
- Identifying the conclusion(s) and further objectives (ie, action points) arising from the meeting; and
- AOB: to include further pastoral enquiry after the barrister, including but not limited to whether the barrister is content with the structure and content of the meeting in question.

The so-called 'SMART' approach is useful here when it comes to identifying practice review meeting objectives. The elements of the SMART approach are as follows:

- Specific – detail exactly what needs to be done;
- Measurable – achievements or progress can be measured;
- Achievable – objective is accepted by those responsible for achieving it;
- Realistic – objective is obtainable; and
- Timed – time for achievements on initiative clearly stated.

For example:

- A good example of a SMART objective would be 'I want to increase my income by 35% each year over the next two years to reach £100,000';
- A good example of a non-SMART objective would be 'I want more clients of the right calibre and type'.

The setting of all practice management objectives requires an appropriate level of preparation, focus and realism. The aim is that the practice management manager and the individual barrister are therefore able to work in harmony. For example, reminding each barrister to make frequent contact with his clients is an important part of any practice management programme and the practice review meeting provides an ideal opportunity to instil the cardinal principle of client care: barrister members should ideally aim to create the same degree of trust and confidence which their clerks aim to support and develop with each barrister's professional clients.

Perhaps the key ingredient of a successful practice management system is the creation and nurture of a genuinely collaborative approach between the barrister member and the practice management team members who run the practice review meeting. It takes both sides to work closely with one another to have a clear sense of what the objectives are and what each side needs to be doing with clear goals and an identified timeline. Working together as member and clerk/practice manager is vital to success. The definition of success could mean different things to different members. Therefore, one must never assume that each member of chambers has the same goals. In the author's experience, that is rarely the case (save at such a level of generality as to be of no use at all – eg, 'making more money'). In any substantial set of chambers, there will be members who (for example): (a) are driven by purely financial goals; (b) have as the sole aim of their professional lives elevation to the High Court bench or beyond; and (c) care not at all for any such matters. Any working practice management system cannot be robotic in its approach and must allow for flexibility and fleetness of foot. Similarly, any goal which is formulated in the absence of a collaborative, realistic and focused plan is doomed to exist only as an unfulfilled wish.

The timing and environment of any practice review meeting should also be tailored to, and therefore appropriate for, the barrister member in question. For example, if the barrister is a single parent, then it will most likely be inappropriate and unhelpful to suggest an early morning practice review meeting. A similar point, but applicable to all barristers, applies to the choice of venue for any practice review meeting – a busy external venue is equally inappropriate in circumstances where confidential information concerning a barrister's practice is to be discussed. Finally, the surprisingly recent times where this type of meeting might have been arranged on an *ad hoc* basis are now gone.

There are two other key points to note here.

- First, practice review meetings should be held regularly but not too frequently: one practice meeting per quarter should suffice. Holding just one meeting per annum is unwieldy both in terms of assessing progress against previously identified objectives (see below) and identifying further objectives which are capable of meaningful review. Moreover, a focused and 'sharp' meeting is far more likely to keep each stakeholder engaged and motivated.
- Second, action points and related 'follow up' acts are of the utmost importance here. The whole purpose of holding such meetings is defeated in the absence of a logical, systematic and accountable approach towards tracking and measuring progress against the strategic plan or objectives identified in the meeting in question (this applies to all such meetings, of course).

2.3 Practice management, client service and business development

In simple terms, the three terms (or concepts) identified in the heading above are fundamentally symbiotic. An understanding of the direct link between these three terms is a key element of any successful chambers' practice management system: if the three do not 'gel', then it is highly likely if not inevitable that they will each operate to a substandard level within the chambers environment.

For example, a highly efficient client relationship management programme will ultimately have a positive impact on repeat business (ie, business development). Equally, even with an effective practice management programme, developing business of any kind will prove difficult if the individual barrister is not providing his clients with an effective service. Barristers now operate in an environment which is openly more competitive, and outstanding client service is essential in order to compete effectively. To assess the quality of client service being provided, in particular at the practice review meeting, it is essential to consider client feedback.

It takes time to obtain, measure and take into account client feedback. Any practice management decisions must be made and based on this feedback. To learn from the feedback, it is important to analyse it realistically and to communicate it effectively to the barrister, and to do so in a positive way, so that improvements or adjustments can be made as required. It is important to get this right, so as not to risk misunderstandings, create false expectations or (worst of all) undermine the clerk/barrister relationship.

3. Business development in a little more detail

Even as recently as 20 years ago, the concept of business development (ie, marketing barristers' services to solicitors) was frowned upon by many at the Bar. It is now universally accepted that this is an essential part of the everyday business of any ambitious chambers. Accordingly, any modern chambers' business model must incorporate some form of business development programme, not least to survive in the hugely competitive (and sophisticated) market via which often complex and multi-layered legal services are delivered. Although unheard of until relatively recently, many barristers' chambers now employ specialist business development professionals to work alongside clerking and practice management teams. If such investment is made wisely, whether by engaging the services of specialist business development professionals or 'training up' internally existing members of the clerks' room, it often provides an efficient way of increasing instructions and therefore improving chambers' revenue.

This investment from chambers is not only about providing the necessary financial support – whether it be hosting networking events for clients or investing in training staff in the importance of business development – but also about providing the right resources and support. Business development can only be successful in a chambers environment if the whole team, members and staff, communicate properly and have the right systems in place to make it effective. This creation of a shared vision is important for a chambers' environment because the business model is made up of self-employed entities rather than a firm in a traditional sense.

Although barristers often work in competition with one another, they do at times need to develop business together at shared client events that chambers will host. It is important that chambers make an investment on a common message or identity that sets them apart from their competitors. This investment must include appropriate business development training for both members and clerks so that there is a common message and a chambers brand is established to enable clients to recognise the benefits of working with chambers. If chambers invests in this message and identifies what it stands for (ie, do we offer higher levels of service than our competitors? Do we offer modern technological services?), whatever this message is it will need to be plugged in to any business development initiatives set up by chambers. A chambers' core brand is important and must be communicated through all channels in chambers – whether that be personal contact with members and staff or through social media sites such as the website, LinkedIn or Twitter feeds. The decisions made on business development initiatives must always centre around a chambers' core brand, and this requires investment at all levels from the chambers' management team.

3.1 The importance of 'staying in touch'

A key focus of business development strategy within any chambers involves an almost religious commitment towards 'staying in touch' with clients. This can be done in a variety of ways and from various sources in chambers (ie, members of chambers or client-facing staff). It is important to stay in touch because with competition at the Bar at an all-time high, rival sets will always be more than happy to step in and develop a competing relationship. It is also important to consider that different people want different things, and some clients simply do not want constant contact or indeed want a different form of communication (ie, no marketing emails and a simple catch-up call each quarter would suffice). As in all areas of practice management, it is important not to be robotic in this important process and allow for flexibility in any approach. In the modern era, there are so many ways of staying in touch with clients, and in a chambers context it is important not to ignore the methods of communication certain clients respect and require. This does not necessarily mean adopting a regular or extensive lunch entertainment programme, which can quickly become out-dated and expensive.

For example, a 'STATOY' (Saw this and thought of you) programme in a chambers environment is often effective because it can be done quickly and from your desk. This type of approach should never replace face-to-face relationship meetings, which are considered in the next section, but should be done in conjunction with an effective relationship management programme. Many of these approaches require a level of common sense, but staying in touch in a chambers environment is a key component of any business development programme. This could be something as simple as noticing that a client's name is not on a delegate list and making contact, or noticing their name on the delegate list for an event that a member is due to attend and writing ahead of time to say that you look forward to seeing them there or perhaps suggesting a drink afterwards. Another example is to make contact briefly with a client recently mentioned in the press.

4. Relationships

As we said in the introduction, as a predominantly referral profession, relationships with instructing lawyers are at the heart of what we do. It should not be overlooked that essentially we are a 'people industry' and therefore the ability to strike up and maintain good relationships is fundamental. It takes hard work and an investment of time to develop and maintain relationships, particularly when barristers are busy on a case, but they cannot afford to neglect this aspect of modern practice. We have seen many successful barristers still make the time to attend or participate in marketing initiatives, even when they are flat out with work. It makes a positive difference.

So how do we go about developing these relationships? Most established sets of chambers will have fostered relationships with law firms, in-house counsel, legal departments of regulators, and individuals within those firms and institutions over many years. While it is important that these core relationships are maintained as a collective and individually, you will want to develop new ones and perhaps revive neglected ones.

One way we have gone about maintaining relationships and staying in contact with key clients is having members of the clerking team act as client relationship managers. Clerks will meet with identified partners and associates or the equivalent every six months for example, and run through a set agenda, which will include items such as cases referred, recruitment of new practitioners, market trends, marketing opportunities and fees. By regularly staying in contact like this you generate a deeper understanding of what both sides are doing and, importantly, what clients want. It also helps to develop a more open dialogue, which can be helpful when dealing with, say, overdue fees or if a member of chambers has come into some unexpected availability due to a settlement or adjournment of a case.

Clerks and members must all accept a responsibility for the maintenance and creation of relationships and be prepared to share them if they are to reach their full potential. No one should have the exclusive control of and access to these relationships. For example, successful clerks will have the ability to make introductions to existing clients of a set. Equally, a more senior member, perhaps a former pupil supervisor, can introduce juniors to some of his professional clients. What is essential is that a culture of strong business relationships is encouraged for the benefit of all. You can never have too many friends.

As covered in the practice management section, the relationship between the member and clerk is important and requires both the clerk and barrister to work together. We like to encourage members and clerks to participate actively in relevant professional associations and networks, including speaking opportunities. Without doubt, networking with fellow professionals focusing on specific types of work has positive benefits. Following up and developing these contacts is of course essential and is likely to form part of the discussion in practice review meetings.

It is never too early to start building meaningful business relationships. I have always been keen to see junior members strike up contemporaneous relationships when starting out in practice and hone their business relationship skills. After all, the juniors and young associates of today are the Queen's Counsel and partners or heads of department of the future. As contacts at law firms or in-house departments progress in their careers, they will have the ability to choose who they instruct and can be influential in the development of a practice. You want to be the person they think of. After all, instructing lawyers can be spoilt for choice so you want to be the barrister that they turn to first.

At the other end of the spectrum, more senior members of chambers need to ensure that they meet and create relationships with up-and-coming partners and senior associates to keep their contact list refreshed, having created a core group of contacts throughout their practice.

Affability is a key component in all of this and some would argue that it can play a bigger role than pure legal brilliance; after all, as the saying goes, 'people buy people'. Ability is frequently taken as read. In one of my former chambers for example, I was once asked by a Vinerian Scholar shortly after he had successfully completed his pupillage what the key to a successful practice was. I replied 'approachability'. As a member of chambers, you want to be the go-to person that an instructing solicitor will turn to for a conversation if they are stuck on a point and need some quick advice and help, which is not necessarily chargeable, but helps in deepening the relationship. The chances are that if the matter goes further, that barrister would be formally instructed.

More recently, this approachability and accessibility has developed further. It is not unusual for members to assist instructing solicitors with whom they have good relationships in pitches that the solicitor is making for new work. It might require investing an hour or so reviewing documents and giving some observations on how the pitch could potentially be improved; however, that hour invested might be the difference between the solicitor winning the pitch or not. If successful, you would expect the solicitor to turn to the barrister who helped him to secure the new case.

It is equally important that clerks are encouraged and empowered by their chambers to create professional relationships with instructing lawyers for them to be most effective both domestically and internationally. As part of an excellence in service offering from chambers, instructing lawyers need to feel that they can turn to a clerk they know well for advice on who the most appropriate barrister is for a new instruction and trust their advice. In some instances this may not be a member from your own set. However, good clerks will have developed strong relationships with clerks from other sets of chambers who will have the specialist skill set that is being sought. Similarly, it is crucial that the clerking team has good relationships with listing officers within the courts and tribunals. This is something that chambers do not charge for, but is critical from a service perspective to professional clients.

So, ultimately, what are we looking for from our business relationships? I would say it is being able to make working life easier, to acquire new work to advance members of chambers' practices in the direction they want, to be able to speak openly with instructing lawyers and members of chambers, and to maximise the enjoyment of what we do for the benefit of clients.

5. Conclusion

For chambers and individual barristers to be successful requires realistic, clearly defined and properly executed strategy. Central to this will be effective practice management and business development, which requires a commitment from barristers and clerks to form good working relationships and to operate as a team.

Good clerks will be able to put the knowledge that they gain about their members' qualities to use when proposing them for new work to instructing lawyers. A vital part of what clerks do is matching the right instructing solicitors to their barristers and vice versa. What we mean here is matching up people that are going to get along. Particularly in long-running matters, it is important that all the lawyers can work as a team and form a respect for each other's abilities. Get this right and the relationship that is struck will lead to future work. It also forms a trust in the clerk's judgement from the instructing lawyer.

As sets of chambers have turned to business development and marketing professionals to drive initiatives, the clerking team has retained its position as the 'sales team'. It is ultimately the clerks who have the most contact with professional clients and it is therefore easier and appropriate for them to strike up business relationships for the benefit of their members. Flowing from this too is the ability to stay in touch, the importance of which we have covered in this chapter.

While email is useful, it is no substitute for verbal and face-to-face communication. These are two crucial aspects required for relationship building and major players in practice management and business development. Honing a strong skill set and overcoming shortfalls in these areas will go a long way towards making you stand out in the crowded competitive market we operate in. As we said earlier, often ability is taken as read by clients, but it is affability that can make the difference. The unique business model that has been referred to in this chapter demands a bespoke approach to creating the right opportunities for success.

International development

David Grief
Essex Court Chambers

1. Introduction

I was delighted to be invited to write the chapter on international development for this book. With a career in managing barristers' chambers spanning over 45 years, the last 37 years being with Essex Court Chambers, I have been in the very privileged position to see, first-hand, the development of the English bar on the international stage.

The Bar may be perceived as the more cautious and conservative arm of the legal profession when it comes to marketing innovation. If you think about the first legal websites, embracing social media, finding budget for commercial sponsorships and many other key marketing developments, the Bar has paused, waiting to see what works for law firms before following suit. However, I think it is a different story when it comes to business development, where the barristers' clerk has arguably been ahead of the game, both in terms of recognising the importance of client and intermediary relationships, and being successful in developing and retaining these bonds.

In spite of this, for many, the idea that the English Bar, the very image of British traditions in the most Dickensian of terms, might have a major role in terms of determining international legal development might seem somewhat out of place and even arrogant. However, as I intend to show in the following pages, the English Bar is ideally placed and perfectly formed to do just that.

2. History

International development of the Bar is not a new phenomenon. The Bar has always been an internationally oriented profession. As the 'common law' originated in England and Wales, English barristers really come into their own in jurisdictions where English law is dominant and they have long been able to appear in the courts of other Commonwealth jurisdictions. The colonial history of England means that there are a significant number of legal systems based, at least initially, on English law.

Barristers are able to provide expert opinions in English law, as well as acting as legal representatives. They can also be appointed as arbitrators, mediators and adjudicators. The number of barristers with international practices is growing all the time, and within every specialist area there are opportunities to develop an international practice.

3. London and the law

London is the leading common law jurisdiction, and so as British colonial history sets up the English Bar to operate across the world, London's modern status as one of the leading financial and commercial centres in the world confirms its credentials as a pre-eminent centre for international litigation and arbitration. Foreign litigants accounted for more than 70% of the cases before the English Commercial Court last year (2016/2017). Transactions of enormous value are conducted in London in fields such as banking, investment, financial services, insurance, reinsurance and shipping. The London Stock Exchange is the most international and largest stock exchange in Europe. More than half of the London Stock Exchange top 100 listed companies (the FTSE 100) and over 100 of Europe's 500 largest companies are headquartered in central London, although as I write we are yet to know what impact Brexit may have on this position. London has a highly developed infrastructure, excellent transport links and is increasingly multi-cultural. To quote London's mayor, it is an international hub of creativity and a beacon of diversity. However, other important factors encouraging the volume of international dispute resolution being conducted in London include the dominance of English as an international business language and the fact that English contract law is the most important and most used contract law in international business. International businesses frequently choose English law to govern their contracts and the disputes arising from them because it is a highly developed system which offers a greater degree of legal certainty than most others. It is based on precedent and relies upon previous decisions. It is usually possible to find answers under English law to the particular legal questions that arise by reference to decided cases and the reasoning applied in those cases.

4.   The independent nature of the Bar

So we have history making English the dominant law and London's success making the location attractive; the final ingredient is the practitioners themselves. The English Bar provides a pool of talent in advocacy and specialist expertise, but barristers have one particular quality which gives them a legal advantage over solicitors on the international stage – their independence.

Barristers' chambers are not 'firms', nor are their members partners or employees. Rather, a chambers is made up of individual barristers, each of whom is a self-employed sole practitioner. Members of chambers are commonly retained by opposing sides in the same dispute, both in litigation and arbitration, with protocols in place to safeguard confidentiality. As well as acting on opposing sides, individuals appear in front of other members acting impartially as deputy judges or arbitrators. This independent status gives the English barrister enormous flexibility and freedom to develop individual practices irrespective of any collaborative strategy of his colleagues. The chambers' 'brand' is simply a wrapper but it does not dictate or restrict for whom or with whom an individual may work. It is the comparative freedom of movement of the English barrister which allows him to develop an international practice with relative ease; the English solicitor must hold back and wait for mergers or alliances.

Having established that the self-employed status of the barrister is fundamental to the Bar's ability and flexibility to work internationally, let us now explore how this provides a context which offers huge potential for English barristers to develop international practices.

The basic principles of international business development are the same as developing any practice – research the market into which you want to move, set achievable objectives, and once you have a good understanding of the challenges ahead, develop an action-based marketing plan. Once you have a toe in the market consolidate with the same techniques you would in a domestic market: be good at what you do; look after your key client relationships and do not let them down in terms of effective communication and fulfilment of promises; develop a reputation for being a 'go to' expert for your area of specialisation; make sure that your target audiences are aware of your expertise through effective marketing communication; and maximise the use of your marketing time with precision targeting, long-term planning and good use of resources available. These principles, which apply to a domestic market, remain true in terms of developing an international practice, but the much larger marketplace offers even greater opportunities than the domestic arena and effective marketers must adopt perspectives to match.

5.   What we can learn from other international professional firms

We can learn from the experiences of other professional firms – the many accountancy and law firms which have had multi-location operations for many decades. These international firms continue to develop international presences in spite of the challenges of establishing workable management hierarchies that provide the benefit of both local autonomy and firm-wide collaboration. You only have to look at, say, the US firms based in London, which continually strive to market locally but with, in the majority of cases, marketing strategy and communications tools being developed by a centrally based US team. All lawyers are wordsmiths and so receiving correspondence written with American spelling when your contact is based in London is, perhaps, not the best first impression. Success is most evident in those firms that have empowered the local practice to create individual business development strategies while encouraging the lawyers on the ground to harness the central resources of the wider organisation but further shaped to reflect the local market.

These multinational firms have bases in key business and financial centres around the world. They may be foreign offices of the one partnership or an LLP as in the case of Clifford Chance or maybe a looser affiliation trading under the one brand as in the Baker McKenzie model. Some firms have entered the market by buying up a small local firm; others establish a presence by manning the new office with ex-pats from London or elsewhere. Whatever the business structure, for a law firm's business development strategy, location is all-important. Not so the English barrister whose place of work, his 'chambers', may provide a physical building to unite members, but it is not necessary for a barrister to have an 'office' in a country in order for him to have a practice, although of course, as members of Essex Court Chambers have proved with Singapore, it can provide a focus and be advantageous in showing a commitment to a region. A brass plaque is not a necessity for a barrister as his international reputation is based on his (and his clerks') ability to maintain relationships with foreign lawyers and his expertise to achieve the results his client expects. Unburdened by corporate structures or potential client conflicts, English barristers continue to be increasingly in demand to provide legal advice all over the world.

6.   **Words matter**

The English barrister's independence allows a chameleon approach to meeting the needs of the global client. We have touched on the advantages of English being the dominant business language, but in terms of business development, it is also important that an individual does not unnecessarily limit himself, or worse alienate himself, from a prospective client with a lack of thought around language and terminology. This is particularly true in terms of how we refer to ourselves in a business development context, especially at the introductions stage. We may be defined geographically by our professional qualifications; an 'attorney' is American, an 'avocat' French and so on. However, all of us can be accurately referred to as 'lawyers'. Universal terminology works well in developing an international practice and so thought should be given as to how you present yourself and consider descriptions such as 'international lawyer' rather than 'English barrister' when seeking opportunities outside the United Kingdom.

What you call yourself is also of relevance when we talk about the role of clerks in terms of business development generally and this is even more challenging in an international context. This is another fundamental difference between barristers and their solicitor colleagues. Professional business development teams within law firms have grown significantly. In the early 1990s even the largest of firms employed only a handful of marketing and business development professionals; today we are talking about highly qualified multi-functional teams supporting every practice area and every office. The Bar has its own growing band of marketing professionals, but when it comes to business development and driving practice-marketing initiatives, it is still very much the role of the clerk, albeit that for many sets, the term 'practice manager' is increasingly being used. Whatever the title, rolled up in the one function of 'clerk' are several support functions common in any law firm. The clerk is the intermediary between barrister and client responsible for relationship management and client care, fee negotiation and administration relating to the management of both the client relationship and the actual day-to-day running of the case. When developing relationships internationally, be aware that meaning can be lost or mistaken in translation and that it is more important that the role and relationship of the clerk as an agent to the international lawyer is understood.

7.   **Understand the differing business cultures**

Being an international lawyer means you are working with a myriad of different business cultures, and if you are serious about developing a place in a country's legal market, it is imperative that you are constantly mindful of different working practices around the world. You need to start with understanding the local legal structures. Never assume that foreign lawyers operate in the same way as English solicitors' firms. Some have structures more akin to a set of chambers, with each lawyer or partner earning only from his own cases. Others pass profits back only to the partner who introduced the work to the firm, regardless of who did the work or where it was done. You need to appreciate the financial incentives of any firm or individual in giving an English barrister instructions. It also helps to recognise that the training and career path for a foreign lawyer does not always mirror that of an

English solicitor, but do look out for shared educational interests as many do spend time in the United Kingdom.

Cultural sensitivity is a key requirement for anyone wishing to be a business player rather than a holiday tourist. Nothing is better than experience but to avoid costly mistakes, research in advance of visiting a country the correct way of doing business with different nationalities. The European Commission has funded a website called 'Business Culture' covering 31 different European countries, but cultural differences can be even more important when dealing with major markets such as China and India. Issues such as negotiation practices, body language and the use of business cards and other aspects of etiquette can be vital in terms of succeeding as an international lawyer.

8.   Opportunities

Opportunities for the independent international lawyer abound. There are currently 193 Member States in the United Nations but probably only a third of these countries are well resourced in terms of legal capability. Even those countries with an established legal market welcome the broader perspective of a barrister with global commercial experience, and on the whole the domestic lawyer looks on the English barrister favourably and as an alliance worth cultivating. There is no conflict of interest in terms of who does what as there is a strict line of demarcation between what a 'foreign' and a 'domestic' lawyer can do. An English barrister does not threaten the role of the domestic lawyer as he is not there to take over the day-to-day caseload; nor is there any incentive to steal the lay client as there is a greater potential source of work from the foreign lawyer himself. Direct access instructions from foreign lawyers continue to be a steady stream of work for the English Bar and are nearly always the first point of entry for a barrister to work in a particular jurisdiction.

The liberalising of the legal profession around the world, with many jurisdictions making it easier for non-domestic lawyers to practice, is also a huge opportunity. This is particularly the case in specialist fields such as arbitration, where the significance of the awards made and the complexity of the disputes, often multinational and cross-border, have led the demand for the ability to appoint only the very best arbitrators. This huge explosion of international arbitration and alternative dispute resolution (ADR) has been one of the most important developments in international law of the past decade and it can be simply explained by the fact that this style of dispute resolution cuts through questions of jurisdiction, moves away from the traditional courtroom setting, engages mediations with a neutral third party and thereby allows the parties, which are often from different commercial and legal cultures, to process the dispute in such a way that all parties feel comfortable with the fairness of the process. As the 2,000 members of the London Court of International Arbitration reflects, it may cover more than 80 countries worldwide but with headquarters in London, it is the English barrister that leads the charge in terms of this specialist area.

9.   What do we mean by international development?

Rather than repeat content already covered in a previous chapter which explores the principles of business development, the following pages are to highlight how some of these principles and techniques can be adapted when your client base is in differing jurisdictions.

9.1   Strategy

A planned approach is advisable but this is quite a modern concept for the Bar. The truth is that for most of my career, developing an international market has been based on a little inspiration, some fortunate introductions and sheer tenacity and determination to travel to meet up with clients and prospective clients at a time when a senior clerk leaving London was considered ground-breaking and even attracted a little bit of gentle leg-pulling!

However, with international earnings of the Bar rising from £90 million to £232 million over the last 10 years, international business development initiatives are now increasingly considered a worthwhile, if not necessary, investment. First steps should always be to establish a strategy. This does not have to be a complex and detailed approach; in fact as a first stage there is a strategy in itself of having no more than one page to put forward a case that will enable you to test the waters in terms of buy-in from members. Subject to individual countries' visa restrictions, English barristers can travel and work on an advisory basis with comparative ease outside the United Kingdom. Although there are not the logistical challenges and practical implications of trading goods overseas as faced by corporates, it is still essential to have an international strategy which is shared and embraced by members. To develop relationships and a profitable stream of work in a foreign jurisdiction requires investment of both members' funding and time.

In developing your case for targeting a particular jurisdiction the obvious question you have to both ask and answer within this one page strategy document is 'why?' A useful technique for providing focus and to test the 'why?' of any strategy is a SWOT (Strengths, Weaknesses, Opportunities and Threats) analysis.

In practice, it is highly unlikely that you will ever start with a completely blank page. The 'Opportunity' column will already have some content as it is nearly always this unplanned spark which provides the impetus for exploring the development of a market further. This opportunity could be:

- a change in the rules such as the liberalisation of a jurisdiction making it easier for foreign lawyers to practice;
- a client opportunity in that an existing relationship and provider of work has non-UK interests and wants to be able to instruct you;
- the prospect of aligning or associating chambers with a potential 'Overseas Associate' as Essex Court most recently did with Gourab Bannerji SA, which met the objective of developing India as a growing source of work; or
- it could be as simple as having a member or a number of members involved in an overseas conference which prompts a cost-effective window to explore the potential of the jurisdiction hosting the event.

If 'Opportunity' provides focus, the 'Strengths' column tests the feasibility of the project. Playing to your strengths is always a wise move or otherwise you may find yourself identifying a great opportunity only to be opening the door for other barristers to reap the benefits.

Having said that, marketing the English Bar, as opposed to just your own set of chambers, is sound business development practice. This is particularly true when marketing in a jurisdiction which does not have a history of dealing with the English Bar – as can be illustrated by a recent business development trip to Zurich. Paving the way for the English Bar as a whole is a sensible first step which can then be followed up by more focused activity to sell in your set of chambers and individual barristers.

Strengths can come in the form of members having an established reputation as a result of past cases, a long-term commitment to raising profile, or relationships in the right places. Essex Court Chambers was perfectly placed for developing a Dubai-based practice because Sir Anthony Evans, a former Head of Chambers, was between 2005 and 2010 the Chief Justice of the Dubai International Financial Centre (DIFC), where English common law reigns supreme.

In getting the right balance in your strategy document you also need to identify any obstacles which might slow down your progress in developing work in a new jurisdiction. You need to be aware of the local political and cultural environment of jurisdictions; there may be countries your barristers will simply not want to visit because of their personal political views, religious beliefs or gender identity. You also need to examine competitor activity and be able to evaluate whether the presence of other English barristers is developing or opening up the market or whether it has reached a point of saturation.

A first step strategy can gauge interest and win the commitment of individual barristers to support future activity. With member support guaranteed you can then proceed to a more detailed action plan. If this backing is not forthcoming, it is probably a case of 'back to the drawing board', as without encouragement from key members of chambers, even the most thought-out strategy is unlikely to succeed. It is also true to say that although the clerks' team may be the drivers behind the strategy, acting as the barristers' 'agent', the prospective client will always want to meet the 'talent'.

9.2 Planning and targeting

International development takes time and it takes money. It is generally the realm of the senior rather than junior end of the clerks' team as it is common, and more cost effective, to travel alone or with one or two barristers visiting for work. Do not underestimate the amount of time it can take to establish overseas connections and to be in a position to recognise the opportunities. I have actively championed and successfully promoted the huge potential of the English Bar in an international context since the 1980s and so believe me when I say it cannot be achieved overnight or as a result of just one or two visits. You can only manage a finite number of relationships and so you have to be selective and you have to be constant. It took many years of visiting Singapore before dividends paid off and work started to flow. You cannot target all countries but need to focus on one or two regions at a time. When selecting international targets, be aware of why you have chosen these jurisdictions and do not forget to play to your strengths.

When you do have an opportunity to plan an international trip, as tempting as it might be, forget the sightseeing in favour of a planned schedule of meetings and hospitality with existing and potential clients. However, pace yourself, as although it is important to get as much out of the time available as possible, dropping off to sleep in a meeting is not a good impression and jetlag is not a good business excuse!

9.3 Relationships – a good place to start

As in the United Kingdom, developing relationships should take priority over investment in developing profile. Both are important, but whereas the marketing efforts which result in a set or individual being known for a specialist area can foster opportunity, relationships produce instructions.

In today's digital marketing world it is easy to be convinced that because you have over 1,500 Twitter or LinkedIn followers or 20,000 website visitors a month, that you have all the relationships needed for an international practice. Do not get me wrong, impressive media statistics do help, but in my opinion, nothing has the impact of a face-to-face meeting and this holds true for a visit to Manchester or Birmingham as it does to Hong Kong or Athens.

The best relationships to assist with international development are those which are already strong. If you have an existing client in a target jurisdiction, it is worth exploring how he might introduce you to other good contacts. A London solicitor client may be able to effect an introduction to his colleagues in an overseas office or at least increase the odds of them agreeing to meet by sending them an introductory email. At Essex Court we have had direct benefits from keeping in touch with members who have taken on international roles such as Dame Rosalyn Higgins, DBE, QC, a former President of the International Court of Justice or, as already mentioned, Sir Anthony Evans, who was a huge influence, because of his role in the DIFC, in the development of Essex Court Chambers' Middle Eastern practice.

9.4 Client care – retaining and developing relationships

It is relatively easy to manage the relationships with your clients and contacts in the city in which you work. You will meet at events, collaborate together on marketing initiatives, speak regularly as part of the process of case management and, if you have not seen someone for a while, an hour out of your day would comfortably cover a coffee and a catch up. It is not so simple with an international relationship base. I cannot practically be in, say, Dubai or Singapore every month or indeed every year, but I can ensure regular communication and follow the interests of my relationships that do have these regions high on their current agendas. This includes keeping abreast of regulatory developments and change through key contacts. It also involves tracking strategic moves of the big firms as well as the less public developments of individual clients with these geographic practices. A good relationship with any client is based on the identification of mutual interests and being able to spot opportunities for each other when swimming in the same pond. It is about keeping your eyes open and your ear to the ground, even if remotely, so that you can add value through anticipation or just pure knowledge. Strong links within a jurisdiction are obviously conducive to a healthy relationship, but other strategies, which are less to do with geography and more to do with attitude, apply as much in the United Kingdom as in other parts of the world. It is simply to do with relationship management practice and the role of the clerk as the 'Middle Man' or intermediary between the client and barrister.

9.5 Getting help – use resources

However, we are not all lucky enough to have access to a broad range of international contacts to help us in developing a presence in a particular jurisdiction. If having a close existing relationship is not your main impetus to develop business within a targeted jurisdiction, there are still a number of resources and business support organisations which can assist you, particularly at the initial phase. The Bar Council is a good place to start as it is actively promoting the opportunities of the English Bar internationally and these initiatives may complement your own endeavours to promote individual barristers or the set as a whole. You might want to consider being involved in the Bar Council business development mission programme which aims to raise the profile of barristers and the legal services they provide in agreed priority legal markets. These missions present opportunities for participating barristers to learn about the legal markets of the visited jurisdiction and to network with local lawyers and other potential clients. The International Committee (IC) of the Bar Council also produces some helpful information which includes the code of conduct rules to be found in the BSB Handbook and the reminder that local rules on conduct may differ, and need to be understood, before accepting instructions from local lawyers. There is some very useful website-based information on the various UK Bilateral Law Associations, which may be of particular interest to dual-qualified members or simply those with family links to a specific country. There are even sponsorship and funding grants available for individuals looking to develop a practice internationally.

It is good to start this research at home but once on the ground in jurisdictions of your choice, do not forget to become involved in local associations. There are great opportunities to sponsor these organisations, which provide an excellent point of entry into the local legal market, both financially and intellectually. For example, having run a student mooting competition with the English Speaking Union in London, we exported the concept to Singapore and we are now in the sixth year of organising the ECC-SAL International Mooting Competition in conjunction with the Singapore Academy of Law. The competition is open to young advocates from Australia, Brunei, Hong Kong, India, Malaysia, Singapore, New Zealand, Pakistan and South Korea, and this has proved an excellent means of raising profile and deepening relationships with young lawyers in all these countries.

9.6 Technology

Without any doubt, advances in technology have been among the greatest drivers in terms of international development. Email has become the main mode of business communication and has made it as quick to communicate with the other side of the world as it is to correspond with the next office building. To speak with someone overseas may require a little forethought to take in time differences, but with advances in conference calling software and the ease of using Skype, even from a mobile phone, it is hard to believe that keeping in touch could get any easier. Technology can indeed enhance business relationships, but to make someone feel that they are important to you there is no substitute for a face-to-face meeting. It is important that technology does not make us complacent or lazy. It is important that barristers who want an international practice ensure that quality time is spent in these selected regions so they can be seen to be part of that local legal community. Equally the clerks need to plan regular business development trips. These visits give a clear message to local firms not only that we consider them important but by meeting me and maybe one or two representative members of chambers, we are able to project a more approachable and less 'ivory tower' image.

10.   Conclusions and top tips

So in summary, the English Bar is ideally placed to develop internationally as a result of the far-reaching influence of and confidence in English 'common law'; the partiality to English as the international language of commerce; London as a recognised legal hub; and finally, the independent status of the English barrister which means that the world is indeed his oyster!

Whether you are reading this chapter as a clerk, a business development professional or an individual barrister, I propose the following as my top six tips for developing an international practice:

- Set out a strategy and get buy-in from key members of chambers. Two or three of the right seniority and skill sets are sufficient to start as others will join as soon as the work starts to come in. This also applies to individual barristers as experience has shown that we are more successful as a 'pack'.
- Always involve members; do not be tempted to go it alone. Prospective clients are happy to talk and negotiate with the 'agent' but generally need to meet the 'talent' before signing the deal.
- The English Bar has a great deal to offer the international legal community but to be successful any sense of superiority must be left at the airport. A truly international lawyer does not have to speak the language but he does need to be sensitive to the importance of terminology and the risks of mistranslation, not so much in the legal documentation but in the communications and cultural exchanges around doing business.
- Airfares may be a great deal less expensive than 20 years ago but it still takes time to travel and so international visits need to be well planned and meetings followed up with a commitment to activity in order to maintain the relationship.
- International clients need to have the same level of client care as those on your doorstep. Embrace the fact that it takes a little more effort to differentiate yourself from the competition.
- Harness the technology that allows you to reach even the furthest parts of the world but remember that face-to-face meetings are still the best way to develop strong relationships.

Marketing and branding

Natalie Hearn
Rachel Murray
Matrix Chambers
Lindsay Scott
39 Essex Chambers

1. Introduction

Barristers form a small part of a large industry. The legal services market in the United Kingdom has a turnover of over £26 billion a year, but in numbers barristers form less than 10% of the profession overall. When it comes to marketing, this presents both opportunities and challenges. Barristers have the opportunity to market to a large, captive professional group (although barristers now have to compete with solicitors in some areas); the challenge is that barristers' chambers, being small groups of self-employed individuals, have to make efficient use of their relatively limited marketing budgets.

Large law firms, which operate both domestically and internationally, employ experienced professionals who put in place large, well-resourced and sophisticated marketing plans that integrate seamlessly with their overall business strategies. They employ a wide range of media tools – websites, blogs, podcasts, seminars, events, publications and social media are the norm. Barristers' chambers need to make themselves heard in this noisy world. They need to attract the cases in an ever-more sophisticated and competitive legal services industry. They have to know who they are, what it is they are offering, and who makes up their target markets. They need to research the best way to retain the clients that they already have, how to attract more work from that client base, and how to expand their client base and their market share.

The key to success is a strong brand, developed through a wide range of marketing tactics which can be leveraged to obtain new work. The danger is that clients, particularly international ones, will see 'the Bar' as an undifferentiated, old-fashioned profession in which quality is a given and the choice of barrister almost random. However, every chambers has the making of a brand – some recent high-profile cases, a reputation in a particular field, a few stars, or some up-and-coming juniors who are being talked about in the market. A good marketing team with a flexible marketing strategy can form these diffuse elements into a strong, clear, instantly recognisable brand.

Marketing should be results-driven, resourced and budgeted. Each barristers' chambers needs to make a decision to properly resource its branding and marketing with time, effort and money. It needs to ensure that its marketing plan is well thought out and in line with, and supporting, its overall business objectives. The marketing plan should cover as many marketing tools/platforms as possible and should be there to support the overall ambitions of the organisation and the barristers within it. It should be an integral and transparent part of the way that the chambers is run.

Part of the plan should be directed at the barristers themselves to help ensure that they are all aware of why marketing and branding are so important, and how it fits into the overall chambers' strategy, and to educate, train and support them in their individual and joint marketing initiatives. It is essential that the barristers are part of the marketing plan, feed into it and assist in every way that they can – be that with content about their cases, articles, blogging, presentations, attending events or tweeting.

Any successful business needs to know that its resources are being efficiently applied. Every chambers needs a brand, and a marketing strategy, but it also needs to know that the resources and money involved are being well spent. Success in branding and marketing has traditionally been hard to measure, but there are now easily available sophisticated tools for measuring the impact of marketing on the audience. New instructions and new enquiries can now be tracked back to marketing strategies and can assist in justifying marketing spend and resources.

This chapter will cover the essentials of marketing a barristers' chambers, focusing in particular on marketing to other professional services. However, many of these principles can also be applied to the marketing of laypersons as part of a direct access offering. It will cover branding, websites, social media and marketing events.

2.   Branding

This section will cover:
- the purpose of branding;
- the elements of a brand;
- the challenges of branding as a barristers' chambers; and
- case example: establishing a new brand.

2.1   The purpose of branding

Many marketing initiatives and efforts would be ineffective without a recognisable brand for your organisation. A chambers' 'brand' is simply defined as a collection of colours, fonts, design elements, tone of voice and key words that represent your organisation. It is not just a logo, but has many smaller elements that can be just as important to conveying who you are.

Your brand should be unique, noticeable and say something about you. All of these criteria are difficult to describe, but can be achieved through consultation and considering the purpose of your chambers. That task is also difficult and requires you to question what people think about you and your chambers. Creating your brand should be a considered and thoughtful process, and a rebrand a serious undertaking. It is (and should be) a time-consuming process, within reasonable limits.

2.2   The elements of a brand

A brand has both tangible and intangible elements.

(a)   Unique

Branding for chambers has additional challenges, which will be explored further below, but one of the foremost is that many have similar key words and numbers, demonstrated mostly by the chambers that are in similar locations: 1, 2, 4, 7, 11, 12 KBW, and also just KBW. Perhaps more than in other sectors, chambers cannot only rely on name recognition to convey their brand, although the combinations of numbers, letters and 'chambers' demonstrate to those who know that you are most likely a collection of barristers. 'Uniqueness' comes from the particular combination of the colour, shape and font of your logo, and the tone of voice.

(b)   *A representation of you*

A common element of all chambers working in a professional services environment is the need to be seen as a professional organisation. This perspective means that chambers' brands overlap, particularly in their use of more serious branding elements, rather than bright colours and playful fonts. More often than not your brand will be competing with dark colour palettes (black, grey, blue, green, white to create space). Similarly, the fonts in our sector are often cleaner, serious and non-cursive.

A more difficult element to create is the tone of voice that represents you – this is the dedicated job of many branding experts and copywriters. However, for many barristers' chambers it is not viable to spend money on external expertise for this. Nevertheless, it is important that the information that describes you reflects the organisation's brand. It should not be the tone of voice of one person – for example, the head of chambers or the chief executive. The tone of voice should be reflected in the content that can be found on any of your marketing materials. You can create this through the types of words, sentence length, the complexity of the content and, more simply, what you want people to know.

Example: For Matrix, a key selling point is our core values. You will find these mentioned prominently on the home page of our website and one of the first things mentioned in our introductory information. This reflects to our clients that we take these seriously.

(c)   *Noticeable*

A challenge for barristers' chambers is to balance recognition with what the elements of a brand say. As described above, it may not be professional to have a logo that is in very bright colours; however, this may get you noticed and in this way you achieve an important part of the purpose of your brand. Again, this is closely linked to the way you want to be seen.

Example: For a long time, the secondary colour in the Matrix palette was a fuchsia pink. While it set us apart, by 2016 we questioned whether it was compromising our professional nature and now it does not appear in our palette.

To be noticeable – particularly in our close-knit sector – competitor audits and an eye on other chambers' brands are a prerequisite to embarking on a brand creation or rebrand. This should also be maintained after your brand is established to ensure there is not accidental (or intentional) infringement of your copyright or trademarks. Competitor audits should extend to law firms and organisations outside the legal sector, with particular attention to organisations that have a similar name to yours.

A brand also consists of the tangible parts that should form part of your deliverables when creating a brand:

- a logo: including a version that does not rely on colour, suitable for black and white publications:
  - usually a word (Coca-Cola), an icon (Apple), or a combination of both (Microsoft); and
  - can contain a colour, shape and font;
- colour palette;
- distance and placement of wording and logos on a page (eg, the Matrix logo generally always appears in the top right hand corner);
- a slogan, motto or subtitle;
- a 'house' font: not necessarily the logo font, or the same one in every body of text or headline, but in these specific uses it must be consistent;
- printed collateral:
  - branded stationery: pens, pencils, notebooks;
  - other branded products: lanyards, mugs, t-shirts – the possibilities on this are endless. However, you should consider the cost of such items balanced with their value to those who receive them;
    Example: At one time, Matrix had branded bubbles and rain ponchos.
  - brochures: for general or specific purposes. This can include company reports (eg, annual strategies) for internal or external publication;
  - commonly used formats such as letterheads (hard copy and electronic), continuation pages, mailing labels, compliment slips, business cards, CV templates (particularly important for chambers); and
  - conference folders and event collateral: banners, PowerPoint templates, biography sheets;
- brand guidelines: a key element of a brand is continuity – without this the recognition and therefore the purpose of your brand is lost. Brand guidelines should cover the small details that ensure use of your branded elements are consistent. For example, it should include the minimum and maximum sizes for your logo and its placement in relation to other elements on the page. It should include an explanation of when to use different types of font and their ideal sizes. The guide should allow anyone in your chambers to understand how to use your brand materials confidently. Do not rely on specific people knowing this information, as we know in chambers jobs can move from person to person and not everyone will be in your employment forever.

(d) *The challenges of branding as a barristers' chambers*

The key tension between a cohesive brand and a barristers' chambers is the self-employed nature of the individuals in chambers. With each barrister working in their own way, and the primary purpose of a chambers to provide administrative support at a basic level, it is difficult to find one voice for this group. However, there has to be an attempt to create one unique voice that supports a brand, for the reasons described above. Sometimes this is easy, as there are moments where barristers come together for a common cause and ethos. This challenge can be mitigated, but investigation and serious thought about your commonalty as a chambers, and finding one thing to connect a brand, should be undertaken. It will be the foundation of your brand, most likely for many years. Shared practice areas, global outlook or location can be enough to make a brand unique, representative and noticeable. Discussion and input throughout the process will assist in creating buy-in for any individual barristers who may not agree with being associated with one cohesive brand.

Case example: establishing a new brand

In 2014, Matrix established a sister brand called Matrix International. Although connected to Matrix's domestic brand, Matrix Chambers, Matrix International had to be built as a separate brand with a different voice that appealed to the international market. The initial process required a competitor audit of other chambers, law firms and organisations which would be providing similar services to us. This served as both inspiration and awareness of what we were up against. Next, our graphic designer interviewed eight or so of our staff and members on what Matrix conveys to them and the words they associate with the way we work. The designer collated these and converted the themes into designs.

3. Website

All businesses must have a website – it is a prerequisite of contemporary business. Barristers' chambers are no different. This section will describe:

- the key features and challenges of a website for chambers;
- the life cycle of a website;
- a suggested course of action for creating a website; and
- analysing use and search engine optimisation.

3.1 The key features of a website

Trends in website development, design and features are particularly fast moving. Any trends listed here will likely be out of date by the time of publication! A chambers' website is also individual to the organisation, reflecting how it would like to be perceived, its brand and reflecting its clients' needs. Therefore, some features are not universal. That said, there are some key elements and challenges that chambers' websites share.

(a) Tone of voice

A website should be an extension of your brand. It should be familiar in the colours, fonts, logo and – most importantly – the tone of voice that your brand conveys. A website is an opportunity to expand that voice and apply it to the detailed content about your organisation – usually branded materials only convey so much and are expensive to update if they need to be reprinted. Therefore, your website is an important way to easily develop your brand as you develop as an organisation.

(b) Browser responsiveness

This is a prerequisite for a modern website. Specific mobile sites are now not suitable in most cases, as a website should be automatically responsive to the size of various browsers (rather than just the size of a smartphone screen). Websites should look as though they are designed and planned for large desktop screens, all smartphones, tablets and various size laptops. Mobile responsive sites are favoured in search engines and allow your users to access your information on the go, when it is likely they would need it quickly and with minimal research. The chambers' contact details should be prominent on mobile sites for this purpose.

(c)   *Informative*

The primary purpose of most commercial websites is a call to action for users to buy products or engage services. For most chambers, their websites have very similar elements, which make it difficult for the organisation to stand out in a crowded market. Chambers have requirements of explaining their practice areas, publishing news, holding information about their barristers and their CVs, and providing contact information. All this information is often wordy, prone to unfamiliar language, and is often inaccessible to a layperson. This tends to make chambers' websites content-heavy. The temptation needs to be to move away from this, and it should be a marketing professional's responsibility to encourage content to be succinct, clear and – crucially – with a crystalised call to action.

(d)   *Call to action*

A chambers' website should consistently and regularly offer its users a way of contacting or engaging in its services. A chambers' contact details are the easiest way to make this call to action, but considering the new ways of communicating, there can be more creative ways of engaging: live chat facilities, newsletters and text services. The method you choose can impact the perception of your services, as accessibility does not always convey the sophisticated nature of legal services, and can cause more contact than resources can deal with.

(e)   *Structure and interface*

A website should have a user interface and structure which is logical – but it is difficult to appear logical to everyone. The sitemap of a website should be carefully thought through and open to amendments in the future and in response to feedback. The structure of the website should include:

- the order of the menu;
- the design of the menu, both at full-size and in responsive mode (where it often collapses or changes design);
- the font size and differentiation between menu items;
- the layout of each page, and particularly the home page;
- the information available on the footer; and
- the path to contact information, or key information to the enablement of your call to action.

This layout should be able to reflect changes and development of your site, even months and years from the launch.

(f)   *Reflecting each barrister*

A key challenge that goes to the heart of our unique business model: while your website requires consistent branding, tone of voice and a singular call to action, it also needs to be flexible enough to allow for barristers to market themselves as self-employed individuals. This is a difficult balance. Often this leads to the compromise of the key features listed above – for example, the tone of voice of a barrister's CV is not that of the organisation, but the barrister. These can differ wildly and appear strange to a user. It depends on the size and nature of your chambers, but the trend should move towards coordinating these voices into one brand for the benefit of all members in a competitive market.

A further key feature that enables the balance between individuality and collective voice is a web development and design team or company that understands the nature of chambers as a sector and yours as its own entity. They should understand that not all designs will apply to all members, and they should assist you in addressing this balance.

3.2   The life cycle of a website

As aforementioned, website trends develop quickly, and it is likely that your website will be out of date in the foreseeable future. A website should be updated every three to four years for chambers, but will likely have to last longer than this considering both financial and staff resources. It should have a plan in place to be maintained in both a technical sense (updates to your platform, which your developers should look after for you), for content (your marketing team should do this on a daily basis), and for wider structure and additions that may be useful for the continued relevance of your website to your users.

3.3   A suggested course of action for creating a website

Developing a website is often a complex and expensive process, requiring coordination of different opinions. A suggested course of action includes:

- considering lessons learnt from previous website development processes;
- a reflection on what works on your current website, and what does not;
- feedback from your key stakeholders:
  - staff;
  - clients;
  - members; and
  - your web development company or designers, which they should consider in their tender or proposal to you;
- a competitor audit;
- an audit of current website trends;
- a meeting of stakeholders to consider the design brief;
- phases of designs, which require consultation with stakeholders (often in the form of a committee of representatives or interested persons);
- sign off on design, sitemap, the form of the templates for the website;
- web development of build of the site;
- initial feedback on the first build;

- beta testing from selected stakeholders;
- communication of launch process and how it will impact the current users of your site;
- the development of a marketing plan around your launch;
- a launch of your website;
- a check that it works as required on different browsers, users etc;
- a maintenance plan in place that covers all aspects of the website;
- analysis of how your website is being used, which should feed in to your maintenance plan; and
- a rerun of the above process within three to four years, depending on resources available.

3.4 Analysing use and search engine optimisation

Your website should be structured in a way that optimises it for analysis by Google Analytics and allows customisation so you can optimise your appearance in search engines. Large companies with greater resources are able to mine this data, which is of continual benefit to their web presence, but in chambers (where staff time is often scarce) this would be unrealistic. However, you cannot allow your website to work with no analysis of how it is visited by your users. It can be useful not only to learn how your users navigate your site (and then changing content or structure based on this), but also for understanding the people and practice areas that are most popular for web users. This often reflects those that have been in the news on high-profile cases, but can bring up some surprises. It can also incentivise members to build their web presence.

4. Social media

This section covers how to:

- use social media to extend your professional network;
- ensure brand consistency across the different platforms;
- set up your profile correctly; and
- implement a social media policy.

Social media offers the opportunity to reach out to existing clients and extend your network by sharing news and opportunities. While it has the ability to bolster a chambers' reputation and showcase members' expertise, when used incorrectly or inappropriately, it can also have the opposite effect. There are numerous social media networks available to use including Facebook, Twitter, LinkedIn, Instagram and Snapchat, to name a few. This section will be focusing on the use of Twitter and LinkedIn, highlighting some of the key advantages, issues to be aware of and tips for making social media a useful business development tool.

4.1 Advantages of social media

When used appropriately, social media has the potential to reach large numbers of people and provides the opportunity to connect with potential clients around the world. By sharing updates and interesting content, social media can direct people to your company website and ultimately result in paid work for members. Unlike more traditional forms of marketing, social media has a wealth of analytics that allow chambers to understand and evaluate the success of individual posts and marketing campaigns. Posts can be altered and shared instantaneously, and this immediacy is particularly useful when sharing real-time news and events.

Clients have come to expect chambers to have a strong social media presence that reinforces the company's brand and provides an insight into the style and culture of the chambers. Individual members who utilise social media can effectively raise their profile on an international scale by highlighting their recent achievements and sharing interesting content.

4.2 Brand consistency

Regardless of which digital platforms your chambers utilises, there should be brand consistency across all of them. This means that when a potential client looks at your website alongside your Twitter or LinkedIn page, they should be able to identify elements of similarity that tie the brand together as a whole. Brand consistency not only relates to the colour schemes in place, but also extends to the language that is employed. As previously mentioned, you should have a set of brand guidelines that specify the company's colour palette, fonts, use of the logo and the style of language.

In addition to chambers having a company profile, all members should be encouraged to create individual profiles and interact with company updates and posts. It may be useful for members to receive basic training on how to set up and manage a profile.

4.3 Setting up a profile

While all social media platforms are different, there are a few basic tips that should be adhered to for both company and individual member profiles. The following tips relate more directly to Twitter and LinkedIn, but the premise can be applied to other social media platforms.

(a) Photo

The profile photo should reflect how you want clients to see you. Images should be high resolution to ensure they are not pixelated and therefore for individual member profiles it is advisable to use a professional headshot. The photo used will help clients to recognise you, so it is important to ensure that it has been taken recently.

(b) Bio

Both Twitter and LinkedIn have a small space to write a bio that should help people to understand who you are and the services that you can provide. Apart from your name, this is the main information that both LinkedIn and Twitter use to pull up profiles in their search function, so all information needs to be clear and concise.

4.4 What content should I share?

Social media is an ideal platform to share articles, blogs and other multimedia content that promotes the work of members. In general, people interact better with visual content rather than purely text-based, so try to use images and videos to grab people's attention. The content you post on social media will only be seen by a small number of your followers at once so content can be recycled and posted multiple times. It is a good idea to try posting at different times of the day in order to reach different segments of your followers. To help you do this, there are a number of scheduling tools that can be used to automatically post content across your social media platforms. Some of these scheduling tools also have the ability to advise you on the best time of day to post content in order to reap the best engagement rates.

In addition to promoting the work of your own chambers, it is more interesting and beneficial for your followers and connections if you also share and comment on other interesting posts. By following companies or individuals that are relevant to your practice areas, there should be a wealth of information that is appropriate and interesting enough to share with your followers.

4.5 Analytics

All of the major social media platforms have helpful analytical tools that can be used to review which posts are most successful and can help to guide future social media tactics. For example, for each tweet Twitter provides information on the number of impressions, likes, retweets and link clicks, and utilises this information to create an engagement rate. When used in conjunction with Google Analytics, these statistics can help to determine how much traffic social media platforms are directing to your organisation's website.

4.6 Social media policy

Creating a social media policy for your chambers helps to provide clear guidelines for staff to follow when engaging in social media on behalf of the company. The policy should include details about the sharing of confidential client or company information and posting inflammatory, illegal or defamatory content. In addition it should encourage employees to interact and engage with the different social media platforms and, most importantly, be delivered in a format that can be referred to and easily understood.

Members who have their own personal Twitter accounts should be encouraged to have a disclaimer in their bio that indicates that all views expressed are their own. While social media can provide a platform for increased exposure to a wide audience, it also has the potential to break reputations. Content shared on social media has the ability to spread around the world in a matter of minutes. Users should therefore be conscious of the fact that the content they engage with will become a reflection of themselves.

Customers can also leave negative feedback on social media which both individual members and organisations must handle with care. Regardless of whether it is a personal or company account, it is important to stay on top of customer feedback to ensure that any negative interactions are recognised and dealt with as soon as possible.

5. Events

This section considers the following aspects of marketing events organised by chambers:

- providing tangible value for both the client and the chambers;
- understanding the purpose of the event; and
- making your events accessible for your target audience.

Events can play an important role in the promotional element of the marketing mix. They provide an opportunity to showcase expertise, network with existing and potential clients, and ultimately provide new revenue streams. There are three main components to organising a successful marketing event: logistics, promotion and content. This section will provide practical advice on organising and running events, as well as highlighting some of the key pitfalls all chambers should try to avoid.

5.1 Defining the purpose of the event

All events should provide tangible value for both the clients and the chambers. When planning an event, it is important to ensure that the type of event is appropriate in order to achieve the desired end goal.

If the purpose of the event is to showcase the knowledge and expertise of the members at your chambers, a seminar and drinks reception may be most suitable. Events that are reactive to topical subject matter and innovative in style are usually the most successful. Alternatively, if the purpose of the event is to get to know a smaller group more intimately, a drinks reception or activity-based event may provide more opportunities to speak to clients on a one-to-one basis. Dependent on the event's purpose, you may find it useful to provide badges to make it easier for members and staff to identify key clients and help with networking.

5.2 Choosing the best date and time

When deciding the best day of the week and time to hold an event, think about your target audience. While an evening seminar or drinks reception may suit certain groups of individuals and practice areas, it is not always the best time for everyone – for example, those who have children or other caring commitments. Try to mix up the timings and days of the week when holding events to ensure that you are not consistently excluding the same group of people. Remember that for certain target audiences an event may not be the most effective way to reach them. Other promotional tools – for example, podcasts and article series – may be more successful.

Always be aware of religious events and school holidays. Make a note of the relevant dates in your event calendar and where possible try to avoid planning any events on these dates. Making your events as accessible as possible is important and reflects well on your chambers.

5.3 Venues

Many chambers choose to hold their events in-house in order to keep costs as low as possible. Dependent on the space available at your chambers, there will likely be events that outgrow your facilities and you will need to look for external venues. Keeping an up-to-date list of available external venues can help to save time, and by developing a relationship with these venues you will find that they are usually very accommodating and will be able to help you with any last-minute queries. Ensure that you have a range of sizes and styles of venues that will suit different types of event – for example, bars or restaurants and conference venues.

When choosing external venues, ensure that they always have disabled access and suitable facilities for your clients. The required facilities will vary depending on the type of event that you are organising, but a few important elements to consider are:

- audio-visual facilities;
- induction loop facilities for hearing-impaired attendees;
- is the venue hire exclusive or do you have a private area?;
- available catering options and minimum spends; and
- cancellation policy.

5.4 Invitation process

Send invitations for events at least six weeks in advance where possible, allowing time for reminders to be sent to non-responders. Attendees appreciate receiving reminders close to the event that include further information and directions. There are a number of online applications which can be used to design and send invitations, and collate RSVPs. These applications help to make your invitations look more professional, allowing you to incorporate your company branding, and helping save time with the management of event attendees. Many of these applications also have the ability to link with the company's CRM system, allowing you to collate further information on clients and keep all of their contact details securely in one place. If you are offering an event free of charge, expect to have a high dropout rate and the number of attendees that you accept for an event should be increased to reflect this.

5.5 Post-event analysis

Following an event, take time to reflect on the successes and areas for improvement. One method of evaluating this is to ask attendees to fill out feedback forms. Feedback forms can be produced in electronic and paper formats and should be short in length in order to encourage attendees to complete them. Including lots of open-ended questions that require written comments can dissuade attendees from completing forms, so try to limit this and instead include four point Likert scales. Dependent on the type of event, it may be appropriate to send a follow-up email thanking participants for attending, providing further relevant information or handouts and, if appropriate, the relevant code for claiming CPD. The follow-up mailing is also a good opportunity to send out an electronic version of your feedback form in case attendees did not have a chance to complete one at the event.

If an event did not go as expected, think about what changes could be made in the future. For example, if there was a poor turnout, try changing the time, format or day of the week. Try talking to some of your trusted clients to find out what they would most value for an event. Remember that there are sometimes elements that you cannot control – for example, the weather.

5.6 Work smarter, not harder

The organisation and running of events can be made simpler by planning ahead and ensuring that you have the right processes in place. One example of this is to create an event checklist where all of the information needed for running an event (eg, location, catering, speakers and required facilities) can be written down. If a checklist is completed correctly, someone who has no knowledge of the event should be able to read it and instantly understand exactly what is required for it to run smoothly. There may be events where the main organiser cannot be in attendance and this checklist is vital to ensure that no information is missed. In particular, if you are using an external venue, make sure to visit it prior to the event to ensure that you are familiar with the facilities and include all of the details in the checklist.

Keeping your client database up to date will help to speed up the process when formalising your guest list and minimise the number of bounce backs received. In addition to formalising your guest list and speakers, think in advance about which other members of staff you will need to help your event run successfully. It is impossible for one person to run an event entirely alone so remember to delegate roles.

Planning ahead and implementing processes for scheduling events, sending invitations and reviewing their progress helps to reduce the stress and workload on the day of an event, and over time it will ensure that your events go from strength to strength.

6. Conclusion

Barristers' chambers that do not market or have a strong brand will not be able to compete in today's legal services market. It is no longer possible for barristers' chambers to rely on the reputation of a few of their barristers or a cohort of traditional clients. In order to maintain market share, a chambers needs to build a brand and employ a wide range of marketing tools. In order to increase that market share and client base, it must do more. It is essential for a barristers' chambers to have a focused marketing strategy that works hand in hand with the chambers' business plans, a well-resourced team, and a brand that will tell the market who it is, what it offers and what it stands for. Barristers' chambers need to compete to differentiate themselves from all the other legal services providers and work hard to retain and attract clients.

Recruitment and talent management

Nick Rees
GRL Legal LLP

This chapter seeks to cover the following topics:

- the history of recruitment at the Bar;
- the evolving world of the Bar and its markets, post the Legal Services Act 2007;
- changing structures;
- the rise of lateral hires;
- the professionalisation of chambers' business and support functions;
- training and development, professional coaching and mentoring;
- technology – best use;
- candidate attraction and retention – selling the business to barristers and staff;
- fair recruitment policies and implication;
- working most effectively with external resources; and
- conclusion.

1. The history of recruitment at the Bar

The Bar can trace its history to the 13th Century and, until more recently, it enjoyed a complete monopoly on the right to represent people in the higher courts. This has now disappeared, with access to the Bar, specialist advice and representation in theory now even easier than before.

Historically, the Bar drew its new barristers from within relatively small and select pools, most often from the affluent upper classes. Pupillages worked in the reverse, with the incoming pupil expected to pay his or her pupil master for the experience, the effect of which was to provide a very narrow path to the profession and of course to limit diversity. To this day, the requirement to undertake a formal pupillage – usually split into two six-month periods, with exceptions being made for those wishing to cross qualify or who can satisfy Bar Standards Boards requirements, where for the first six months individuals are not permitted to undertake court work, but can in the second sixth – remains. However, one of the most significant shifts has been in attraction, with sets now openly vying for the best talent at an early stage. With this competition, financial rewards and openness about chambers and their working practices have increased – at the time of writing, leading commercial set Fountain Court Chambers has released a video showing its inner workings, aimed firmly at the stars of the future. The gloves are off.

Recruitment of staff has also changed significantly. The original chambers model

– where sets were often single-figures of members rather than today's mega-sets and included a senior clerk employed to oversee and manage all elements and aspects of chambers' non-legal business – has gone.

Previously, the senior clerk was responsible for the clerking and practice management, administration, finance and hiring and firing. Members of chambers paid a percentage to the senior clerk and he, rarely a she, ran all the major business functions, including staff, paying from the monies received and with the balance effectively his to keep.

As the world has changed and the Bar has adapted, these practices have almost completely disappeared, although senior clerks on a percentage of chambers' receipted fees do still exist and some still retain considerable control and power.

As the Bar has evolved, so have chambers' staffing teams, with larger groups of barristers – now often 100 plus and working across multiple practice areas – requiring a sophisticated approach to business. Staffing teams are larger than ever, moving from the traditional clerking model to streamlined structures usually split into clerking/practice management, administration, finance and IT. However, the most significant shift has been the rise of business development and marketing, with entire teams now tasked with the promotion of the business and individual barristers and teams. There is of course significant overlap and many of the most successful and highly prized individuals have developed an array of skills allowing them to seamlessly cross practice management with business development; however, the fundamental skill is still people management.

Having been a profession where progression was through 'dead man's shoes', and seemingly the only route forward was by waiting for someone to fall from their perch, clerking and practice management is more competitive than ever. Top talent is in demand and although we have seen an influx of individuals successfully coming into chambers as 'outsiders', often at the CEO or director level, those with considerable experience and a successful track record of working shoulder to shoulder with the Bar and its clients and with a nose for business are highly prized.

Attraction and retention of skilled staff is becoming more sophisticated and more hotly contested. With the Bar willing to offer significant rewards, including bonuses and, increasingly, benefits packages, it is having to fall in line with other business sectors.

This chapter will consider some of the historical reasons and market forces responsible for the changing landscape of recruitment and talent management at the Bar. It will also identify strategies and methods now being used in the market to try and ensure success.

2. The evolving world of the Bar and its markets, post-Legal Services Act

The Legal Services Act 2007 looked to reform the way legal services in England and Wales were provided, including enabling alternative business structures (ABSs), which allowed different lawyers and non-lawyers to form businesses together and permitted non-lawyers to be involved in the management or ownership of legal businesses.

In 2015 the first ABS was attached to a barristers' chambers, 7 Harrington Street Chambers based in Liverpool. Since then, take-up has been relatively slow, but the number of alternative models is increasing. Chambers are using them to attract direct access work, often quietly so and as not to tread on the toes of current clients, seeking work from big business, SMEs and savvy individuals. Certain areas of practice lend themselves more easily to the model; with immigration, property, family, corporate crime and tax being some of those forging ahead.

There has been a marked increase in the interest in new entities by those seeking to step away from traditional models and create 'barrister-led entities' – again, these have thus far been relatively focused, but as the market and, in particular, the use of technology and the rise of knowledgeable clients increases, these become more relevant in the market.

As this chapter goes on to discuss, senior managerial and business development roles at the Bar are now being undertaken by a more diverse range of individuals and often with broad skill sets. As the Bar and its business models become more varied, this is only set to increase – be they working under a classic or more modern approach. The requirements for, and ultimately arrival of, new and highly skilled individuals is likely to have a major impact on how the Bar thinks – especially in areas such as the recruitment of new members, staff and the management of talent.

3.   Changing structures and new roles

Barristers' chambers have been on a long path of transformation over a number of years, with a changing business world, evolving technology and shifting client needs all influencing how sets are run and structured.

We have also seen roles increasingly change – chambers directors, directors of clerking, directors of client care, not to mention business development and marketing professionals forming dedicated teams focused on client service, are all commonplace in chambers now.

One of the real transformations has been the structure of chambers and, ultimately, we are seeing sets streamlining how they are organised. A traditional stumbling block to change has often been the chambers' constitution. These have previously been too static, outdated and less than versatile, often acting as the Achilles' heel to change. Many sets have recognised this and are working with newly written documents which are fluid, more regularly updated and change with the requirements and demands of the business.

Traditional set ups of 'one member, one vote' cast across a wide range of issues is also outdated and can really slow down any resolutions. Largely this is an ineffective and sluggish process which can be exacerbated by management committee meetings generally falling monthly or less frequently, meaning it can be several months before a final decision is made and where lost impetus may not deliver the best result for chambers.

Allowing barristers to vote is of course a democratic way to run a set, but this approach is often flawed. It is often physically impossible to get everyone together and although technology has helped move things on – some chambers now use innovations such as electronic voting – it can still be a lengthy process which could see barristers ultimately voting on a decision which they might not be very well informed about or the outcome might have little bearing on their working life.

As mentioned, roles in chambers have evolved dramatically in recent times, and with the advent of more professionals entering sets in managerial and business development roles, we have also seen more professional structures introduced. The slicker sets are thinking about their decision-making processes and adapting their structures to streamline and refine their businesses.

There needs to be strong and progressive leadership, affirmation of shared values, a sense of togetherness and a clearly defined and documented approach to strategy – not all of which are easily achieved by a collective of busy independent professionals.

One of the ways barristers have been restructuring their decision-making processes is by creating committees and groups with more focus and much greater powers. This has been particularly apparent with chambers' recruitment processes, where some have been able to significantly reduce decision times – often decisive where an applicant is in multiple processes. For many sets it can be nigh on impossible to have everyone vote on a potential new member or members, and this can mean good people are being lost in long-winded process. Creating committees with greater powers to say yes or at least make strong recommendations makes the process much more refined – this also means that we are seeing relevant members deciding on issues which impact them (eg, recruiting barristers in their own practice areas). However, to make these focused committees viable, they must be empowered and trusted to make decisions, allowing for a final decision quickly.

Creating committees can also be a great way to boost buy-in from junior members and involve them in the decision-making process from an earlier stage.

Working parties are another method of speeding up processes. With powers to consider, review and provide answers rather than being required to report 'findings' back to a management committee, such parties can dramatically reduce turnaround on prominent issues and projects. Budgetary control is also used to speed up decisions; where costs fall within pre-set budgets, these can be agreed quickly, thus removing the requirement for potentially lengthy review and sign off from others.

However, there are several pitfalls to consider when adapting a chambers' structure. Ultimately, this is a process which cannot be rushed. It is imperative that if any group which will have significant decision-making powers is created, the right people are involved. There is also a risk that barristers might feel left out of the decision-making process if they are no longer being asked to vote on what they might consider to be key decisions – there is no doubt that many a crucial decision is best discussed face to face. Introducing a new structure requires a sea change and it can be difficult to change minds where a considerable group might feel the current structure is effective.

A lack of understanding about how roles work in chambers could also be a hindrance when introducing a new structure – it is important that everyone's roles and responsibilities are outlined clearly. It is also important not to adopt a 'one size fits all' approach, taking time to work with individuals and groups, recognising strengths, weaknesses and agreeing appropriate definitions of terms such as 'success'.

For many sets, working in teams was initially introduced as a client benefit – creating teams which appealed to customers and their needs. Now we are seeing these teams creating a wider business benefit, enabling sets to approach work in a more analytical way. With this structure in place it can be easier to see where work is coming from and where it is going, as well as looking at service levels and client responses.

A key element to adapting a structure is giving ownership to barristers and staff and sharing responsibility, showing individuals what they are personally contributing. Interestingly, in some sets this is also coming with related targets, which are clearly defined for employees. At this stage such targets are loosely defined for members and are often agreed on an individual basis rather than imposed; thus we are yet to see how targets are to be enforced and this could take another two or three years. However, it is a careful line to tread – although targets can help to evaluate outcomes and create a more sophisticated way of measuring success, targets are not the reason many came to the Bar. Managing and enforcing targeted ways of working is a challenge and one which must be considered prudently – as ever this needs careful handling.

Ultimately there is no one right answer when it comes to introducing a new structure and sometimes restructuring can have elements of failure. However, it is important to evolve – even if that means being prepared to get some things wrong; otherwise sets are in danger of being left behind.

4. The rise of lateral hires

In recent years we have seen an unparalleled number of barristers moving chambers. Switching in this way has of course been commonplace among solicitors' firms, but was previously frowned upon at the Bar. And understandably, given the unique structure of chambers and the nature of barristers' working relationship with their set, leaving can be significantly more complex than departing a business or law firm. Indeed, *The Times* recently reported that some barristers are experiencing large financial penalties for leaving, with some facing bills of up to £50,000 to cover the room and other expenses and a percentage on work that has been billed and will be collected by chambers.[1]

Trying to confirm exactly why the market has changed is difficult. There seem to be several factors at play; some are simply market changes and requirements to meet and satisfy an increasingly diverse set of client requirements – this follows in line with the law firms and changes to their own working practices or client offerings. If a significant client suddenly creates a new department or starts to service an additional area of the market, chambers are now reacting accordingly.

Also, the Bar has become more competitive. Junior barristers in particular are less likely to sit and wait for work or opportunities to find them; where it appears there might be better opportunities in another set, individuals and teams are now more willing to act.

There are of course complications – determining which work will follow, re-establishing and pushing on practices in new environments, new colleagues and new

---

1   www.thetimesbrief.co.uk/users/39770-linda-tsang/posts/19854-lateral-hires-in-the-bar-how-moving-chambers-could-cost-you-50-000.

ways of working, and often intense senses of loyalty all make the process far from straightforward.

However, despite any perceived complications, lateral hires show no sign of slowing down. It has become so common in fact that in June 2017 the Bar Council reviewed professional obligations that might be engaged when a barrister joins or leaves a set of chambers or when an internal dispute arises.[2]

In this review, the committee acknowledged that often "moves give rise to questions about the responsibilities owed by both barristers and chambers" and went on to state that often it is not in a position to settle these disputes and that it "envisages that all chambers will have a constitution and the mutual responsibilities of chambers and departing members should be addressed in this document". However, the committee outlined principles of good practice when a barrister departs.

These include the set clearly stating in its constitution a minimum notice period which must be served by a departing barrister, citing three months as a typical notice period. Looking at costs, it recognises that often a barrister will choose to leave immediately and as such will be liable for a number of months of expenses. It advises barristers to take care not to find themselves in a position where they have to pay expenses as a percentage of fee income to their former and new chambers. Generally, it is highly advisable that chambers' constitutions are clear on this point – while it might be tempting to tax a departing member, it could scupper recruitment plans if the terms are unfavourable.

5.   Professionalisation of chambers' business and support functions

Significant changes in the management, development and support of barristers' chambers are set to continue. If we consider how the Bar looks today compared to 10 or even five years ago, it is now commonplace to have professionals undertaking a range of new roles, from chief executives, chambers directors, directors of clerking, directors of client care to business development and marketing and events managers, all of which often overlap with the traditional role of the clerks' room.

So where does this leave the role of the clerk? Of course, there remains a huge requirement for clerks, but there are several interesting factors behind why this role has changed so significantly.

First, many sets are now organised in a different way – around 20 years ago the commercial Bar started to adapt its structures to better reflect the clients it was serving and to help ensure it was approaching business in a more strategic way. One of the first changes was to create new roles including chambers director and CEO. Today, many sets are willing to look far and wide to find the right people for these roles. For example, it is common to team senior clerks with managers from a professional services background and, usually, the CEO of a set today is a generalist – they have a whole array of management skills, sometimes in unrelated sectors, but importantly they have the people and networking skills, as well as the commercial nous to help a set in this competitive market. Of course, the Bar has not completely

---

2   http://barcouncil.org.uk/media/424039/joining_and_leaving_chambers__and_internal_disputes.pdf.

moved away from a traditional, hierarchical leadership model and many sets still operate with a head of chambers or senior clerk in charge.

Attracting and securing work have also influenced how sets are structured and the role of the modern clerk. For instance, we have seen more work undertaken by solicitor advocates and in-house lawyers and, likewise, some barristers have seen work come directly through lay clients.

The Bar is not immune to the impacts of the digital era and, in particular, the role social media now plays. Marketing is now vital to most chambers, alongside broader business development activity. Individuals at all levels are expected to attract and retain business, and many clerks are now in hybrid roles, blending tradition with sophisticated marketing and business development skills, properly qualified to tackle this new role.

So, what makes for a successful support function in this more modern age? A successful set seeks to marry the traditional elements of the Bar – quality, service, specialist knowledge – with professionals capable of managing business, understanding and controlling finance, and delivering business strategy and significant business development and marketing programmes. In order to achieve this, it is important the Bar recognises the strength of a diverse, well-trained and supported workforce, providing the tools for them to deliver in partnership.

6. **Training and development, professional coaching and mentoring**

With the professionalisation of the Bar we have also seen more of a focus on training and development within chambers.

This has partly been stoked by the changing structures of sets and the creation of roles – many individuals in support and business development jobs have found that they have had to invest in their careers by upskilling. Many are undertaking additional or further education in an associated area or through one of the Institute of Barristers Clerks' programmes of education. Others, looking for an edge, work with dedicated business coaches, who can help to work through new or additional responsibilities or simply act as a neutral sounding board, which has been normal and acceptable practice in the business world for many years.

From the most junior to the most senior role, individuals are now expected to attract, retain and develop business and professional relationships. And of course it is not only those in support roles – barristers too are expected to be adept at business development. Partnering with consultancy 10½ Boots, the Bar Council offers bespoke training for barristers, clerks and administrative staff focused on answering questions such as: how can chambers win work more efficiently and effectively? How can barristers compete more easily in a more competitive environment? And, how can you win more instructions from events, seminars and networking with solicitors?

Positively, we have seen that individuals have taken the bull by the horns, becoming degree qualified, MBAs and chartered marketers, and forcing themselves into hybrid roles such as director of clerking and practice director, combining overall strategic leadership of the clerking and staffing function with significant business development undertakings. This is to be applauded.

Barristers are also increasingly willing to recognise the benefits of coaching and mentoring – not easy in such a competitive market, where this type of support may traditionally have been seen as a weakness.

The Bar Council has developed a mentoring skills course to support all those who are considering or currently mentoring in any scheme across the Bar. The introduction of this course, run in conjunction with an external consultancy, recognises the growing number of chambers introducing mentoring programmes which support not only pupils and junior barristers, but also more experienced barristers. The aim is to upskill those wanting to become better mentors and it covers topics such as techniques in building rapport, establishing mentoring boundaries and setting yourself up for success as a mentor.

Chambers are increasingly focusing on training and mentoring in-house: a positive move which improves a set's retention rates and can help to attract new members and employees too.

7.   Technology and best use

You simply cannot ignore the impact of technology in the business world and the Bar is no different. The proliferation of social media in the business world has been fairly rapid when you consider that LinkedIn was established around 14 years ago and Twitter only 11 years ago. These platforms are still relatively new, but businesses across the board have certainly embraced social media and many use the platforms to great effect. And they would be silly not to, with 328 million monthly active Twitter users and 467 million LinkedIn users worldwide (statistics from Statista).[3]

And it is not just a place for consumer brands or people to share photographs of their breakfast – many legal businesses have really harnessed the power of these platforms, radically changing the way that business development is carried out. According to research from Propero Partners, 90% of those lawyers surveyed have a firm LinkedIn profile and 84% have a Twitter account.[4]

Many legal professionals have harnessed the power of online to produce must-read content – be it on blogs or social media platforms. For example, the UK Human Rights blog, run by barrister Adam Wagner, has been nominated for numerous awards and pulls in around 100,000 page views each month.

We have certainly seen the 'fear-factor' around social media lessen among many barristers. As the so-called 'Millennials' join the profession it is also natural to see the use of social media increase – this is a generation much more comfortable with interacting and sharing information online.

It is fair to say that most law firms have firm-wide social media accounts and for the individual lawyers who tweet, there is usually a social media strategy in place to ensure that lawyers are using the platforms appropriately. As always with these sorts of innovation, there is a disparity and we see some firms engaging with social media in a more proactive and creative way, with others simply doing the bare minimum.

---

3   www.statista.com/statistics/282087/number-of-monthly-active-twitter-users/. www.statista.com/topics/951/linkedin/.
4   www.lawgazette.co.uk/law/two-thirds-of-law-firms-dissatisfied-with-new-business-enquiries/5061256.article.

However, generally, it is fair to say that law firms are alive to the benefits and opportunities that social media can create.

In contrast, for a chambers it can understandably be a little more problematic to ensure consistency in message and tone as individual barristers, if engaged with social media, will tend to have their own ideas about how they want to cultivate their online presence and how they use the platforms to gain a following and potentially win work.

However, although there are more challenges facing barristers' chambers, there is a way to harness social media and control the messages being pushed out online. As with many things, education is key. It is worth organising internal training to explain the social media strategy and outline how members of chambers and staff can get involved with social media and contribute to the set's overall aim. It is certainly a worthwhile activity – a strong online presence can boost brand, help to attract clients and, importantly, assist with a set's recruitment.

Encouraging the sharing of information is also important. Inevitably sets will have individuals who are more familiar with Twitter and LinkedIn – it is important to encourage these individuals to share their top tips and how they make it work for them. A collaborative and collegiate approach will help to foster online success.

But what are the related risks and rewards of engaging with social media? First, let us tackle the risks. Of course, mistakes happen all the time, just as they would in real life, at a networking event or a cocktail party. Recent cases such as *Monroe v Hopkins* [2017] EWHC 433 (QB) serve to shine a spotlight on the dangers of tweeting in a cavalier way – this libel action over a tweet sent by Katie Hopkins resulted in her having to pay Jack Monroe £24,000 in damages.

Likewise, barristers should be careful how they describe themselves online. This was brought into sharp focus this year after the Bar Standards Board delivered a £1,000 slap on the wrist to a leading Queen's Counsel for describing himself on his website as the "UK's top criminal barrister", among other claims. The Bar Standards Board deemed these assertions as "likely to diminish the trust and confidence which the public places in him or the profession".[5]

It is not uncommon for a barrister with a very strong social media presence to see work coming directly from these platforms from lay clients. Of course clients like to work with a lawyer with legal skill and a commercial mind, but, equally, people also like to work with friendly individuals or, more relevantly, those who are 'social'. Social media allows personality to shine through, in addition to creating a place for successes and high-profile wins to be promoted. Clients are savvier than ever and a quick search will reveal whether a barrister has a social media profile, and for some individuals this may well sway their decision.

We are also seeing social media affect how chambers are structured, with specific roles being changed or created to ensure that social media is ticked off and adequately looked after. For clerks in particular we are seeing this role diversify, with individuals in these roles expected not only to carry out the traditional clerking jobs, but also to include significant marketing and business development in their role (as discussed previously, in Section 6).

---

5   www.tbtas.org.uk/wp-content/uploads/hearings/3587/Outcome-Posting-Wolkind.pdf.

Many chambers which are still operating more traditionally and seeing quality work come through the door may well ask why they need to engage with social media, when they are not losing out on work. However, it is still important that sets have a cultivated, rather than organic, online presence. As discussed previously in this chapter, by failing to engage with social media an organisation is running the risk of individuals running riot and posting inappropriately or in a tone that is not in keeping with the set's reputation and brand.

Equally, it is important to avoid complacency – a number of chambers are engaging well on social media, and failing to have a seat at the table can only be detrimental to a brand. Platforms such as Twitter and LinkedIn are not fads and will not go away – they are very much established as part of the marketing mix and it is better to engage sooner rather than later. Failing to have a good online presence might also impact future recruitment – the younger generation of lawyers will naturally check a set's social media channels and some may well be less keen to join if they perceive the brand to be less 'switched on' and innovative.

8.   Candidate attraction and retention

Although the idea of laterally hiring barristers and staff is still a relatively new concept at the Bar, with staff moving between chambers more often, this is changing.

From the Bar's perspective, there has been a noticeable shift from the traditional powerbase of the senior ranks to the young Bar, who are determined to drive change and to do so quickly and effectively.

This is often heightened for some; with university and tuition fees, significant levels of debt and the downward pressure on the availability of work and fees, particularly public funding, the junior Bar is simply no longer willing, or able, to sit and wait it out without structured planning and clearly defined career routes.

The effect of this has been the increasing willingness of barristers, juniors and increasingly silks, including silk-led teams and groups, not to simply stay put in a chambers in which they may have spent a significant amount of their career already. If they feel they are not receiving value for money or the appropriate attention, promotion or professional support, they will look to move on.

The importance for chambers to have certain elements of its business in the right place and shape cannot be underestimated. Unless there is a non-professional reason for moving, a lateral hire at the Bar will be most interested in the quality of business development services, the set's strategy and future plans, and the quality of the clerking and staffing teams – most will put significant emphasis (and in some cases this can make or break such moves) on the strength of the management team, its personnel and their approach to business.

To be successful at the modernising Bar it is paramount not only for lateral hires, but for the retention of current members that a chambers has and can draw on effective business development strategy and plans. It is also vital that those tasked with leading, managing and delivering the non-legal element of the business are highly skilled and credible.

With regard to staff, we are also witnessing a significant shift in approach, driven in part by the increasing use of technology. As chambers' staffing requirements change and become more diverse, the attraction of appropriate individuals has also changed. This might also be attributable to the so-called Generation Y or Millennials, who are often unwilling to step into roles which are poorly defined and have little chance of progress or training.

Again, to be best placed to attract and retain the best talent, chambers must ensure they are in tune with the requirements of the individual and the current market. It is no longer the case that simply the name and reputation of a set are enough. With a broadening candidate pool and a chase for top talent, the assumption that this will be sufficient is misplaced.

The process must begin before a role is even put into the market. Chambers must ensure and place great emphasis on its own offering, what it does best, selling itself through effective communication and of course branding: how appealing is its offering? What does it say about the business and does it deliver the required message? To do so most effectively, it is worth trying to put oneself in the place of a prospective candidate or applicant. Much like the Bar's more recent requirements to appeal to a broader client base, including the direct access client who may have no idea about chambers, its business or its reputation, an informative website and careers page is important.

Another essential element is the idea of brand association – does the chambers' brand or the way it positions itself in the market or even the way it talks to the outside world fit with me? If it does not or the message is confused or antiquated, what does this say to a potential lateral hire or potential new staff member? There needs to be greater emphasis on this than ever before.

More specifically, recruitment processes for lateral hires and staff must be efficient, well presented and above all transparent and fair. Candidates are more likely to join an organisation if the business moves quickly, is decisive in its dealings and ensures the individual or individuals feel valued and wanted. These points are often overlooked or not really fully understood.

9. Fair recruitment policies and implication

With a heightened focus on gender equality and diversity across the business world, it is of course important that chambers are putting in all possible measures to ensure that recruitment is fair and, more broadly, that all barristers feel respected and equal at work.

Since 2012, when the Equality Rules of the Bar Standards Board Handbook came into force, it has been a requirement for chambers to produce an equality policy and action plan, appoint an equality officer, ensure chambers' selection panels are trained in fair recruitment, conduct diversity monitoring and analyse the data, and produce anti-harassment, flexible working, parental leave and reasonable adjustments policies.

These measures were introduced with a specific focus on women at the Bar and there was further progress in 2017 when the Bar Standards Board approved proposals to allow barristers to take advantage of shared parental leave.

For a chambers to ensure it is retaining talent and attracting the right candidates, it is advisable to be open about its equality policies and the measures it has in place to offer benefits such as flexible working.

We are also seeing an increased focus on wellbeing, with the Bar Council recently issuing its first certificates to recognise efforts made to improve wellbeing in chambers – from introducing new policies and initiatives, to small but positive changes such as a mindfulness class or chambers tea sessions or external support.

While it has been true in the past that barristers have trailed behind other legal businesses concerning staff wellbeing, recruitment and retention, they are certainly making great strides now.

10. Working effectively with external resources

Although the use of external resources for advice or support with recruitment, search or HR consultancy projects is not completely foreign to the Bar, it has often been normal practice for chambers to undertake all or most of this themselves, often with mixed results.

As the Bar and its markets become more sophisticated and more demanding, requiring the management of the business to be undertaken by an increasingly diverse group of highly skilled individuals, the importance of getting this right has never been more apparent.

Of course, as well as the need to secure the most suitable individuals, there are often several additional factors to be considered, including costings, timing, the focus and drivers of role and, importantly, the business and its requirements.

For some, working with external specialists is an unnecessary or even unwanted expense, but with such rapid change in the delivery of legal services, directly affecting the Bar and requiring staff to be armed with new skills in addition to those of traditional clerking or practice management, a clear case for seeking expert advice can be made.

In choosing the most appropriate resource, a business must consider several factors internally: budgets, timing, what the role will be tasked with (often influenced by whether the position is newly created or existing), company policy and the overall strategy of the business and future plans. Externally, considerations might focus on current relationships, supplier reputation, costings, timings, market position and levels of trust.

If we consider a senior leadership role in a barristers' chambers, which is often one which requires support from external resources, there are several 'good practice' points to follow.

- Create a committee or group to deal with the recruitment requirement, empower them and ensure they can make decisions – not necessarily the final decision, but to agreed levels.
- Create written plans covering the stages of the process and map out a rough timeline – even where a potential candidate has a significant notice period, a period of handover will be required and notice periods can vary significantly.
- Seek out the assistance of a relevant supplier. Task one of the group with conducting market research and invite more than one company to pitch. Ensure as many of the panel attend those meetings as possible and ask for all

documentation in writing. Seek sample job descriptions, person specifications and ask for detail around recent projects. Take up references and ensure companies outline their full recruitment process – this is vital as once they start to interact with potential candidates, your brand is on the line and it is important to create good first impressions. Negotiate on the price and confirm what it covers and what you get back if the person leaves within the first few months.

- Once on board, work closely with the chosen company. Ask it to map out the process and agree this. Ask it to review any job descriptions and person specifications, agree those and appropriate adverts and placement. Agree a complete timetable, including how the selection and interview process will be run and completed, and insist on regular feedback during the process.
- Once the time for the advert or promotion of the role has been completed and the company has met in person and conducted its own interviews with suitable individuals, meet and ask to be walked through the longlist. Agree a shortlist and arrange interviews.
- Interviews should always follow prescribed best practice and ideally be controlled by a designated chair. For senior positions, interviews might also include a presentation. Best practice is to have all candidates seen on the same day and the entire process completed, to the point of consideration.
- Select candidate and make offer. Once offer is made and accepted, ensure detailed feedback is provided to all unsuccessful shortlisted applicants as quickly as possible.
- It is also very important to outline and confirm the appointment to the individual's new colleagues and staff, not only the lawyers.
- Watch on as news of your immaculate recruitment process, successful conclusion and powerhouse of a new senior staff member sweeps the market and your business becomes the talk of the town.

11. Conclusion

In conclusion, there has been a remarkable sea change in the Bar's approach towards recruitment and retention of its lawyers and staff. Some of this can be attributed to changing recruitment and HR practices, and shifts in legal and contractual requirements, but most noticeably, and with increasing momentum, change is being driven by diversification in the Bar's business model.

Most of this change is to be applauded: best practice recruitment standards, equality and diversity, open discussion about historical gender and social inequality have all played a positive part, but there is still more to be done.

The Bar has become – or, to pacify the purists, has now taken on most of the facets of – a fully blown business. Many barristers and their chambers are now successfully undertaking types of work they might never have considered 10 years ago and there has been real success in the Bar establishing its business in foreign jurisdictions and markets, supported by global recognition of its quality, value and what its stands for and represents.

The next 10 years will see the Bar diversify even further; the rise of technology will not only change the customer experience and relationship, but also create new positions and of course make others defunct.

Whatever the changes that lie ahead, for the most part each business will still be managed, and have its revenues generated, by people. Although technology will play an ever-increasingly important role in the delivery of legal services, including for the Bar, there is no doubt that people will respond most positively when they feel included and are treated like human beings.

Women in law

David Barnes
Atkin Chambers

The power I exert on the Court depends on the power of my argument, not on my gender.
Justice Sandra Day O'Connor (the first woman to serve as an associate of the United States Supreme Court)[1]

The issue of gender diversity within the legal profession has been debated for too many years. In 2017, some 98 years after the Sex Disqualification (Removal) Act 1919, you would have thought that the debate about gender equality would be long dead. Much has been written about it and, in recent years, many steps have been taken to address it. However, the topic remains very much alive. Having been a barristers' clerk for 34 years I have seen much progress in the demographics of the Bar, with a substantial growth in the number of women being called, finding pupillage and, ultimately, obtaining tenancies within chambers. Yet we still have a problem. The notion of empowering women is, I am pleased to say, in the most part long gone. Women are empowered. It is a cultural change that is needed – not just at the Bar, but in society as a whole. Yet the challenge remains as to who is going to advocate for and implement that change. It cannot be women alone, as they will encounter the usual resistance from those around them. Both men and women need to join forces to combat embedded behaviours, and momentum is absolutely key to achieving this.

Before we look at the specifics of the Bar, I think it is useful to look at an example of where this is already working well in the international community. May 2016 saw the launch of the Equal Representation in Arbitration Pledge, which stated:

The Pledge seeks to increase, on an equal opportunity basis, the number of women appointed as arbitrators in order to achieve fair representation as soon as practically possible, with the ultimate goal of full parity.

The co-chairs, Sylvia Noury of Freshfields and Wendy Miles QC of Debevoise Plimpton, have formed an impressive steering committee made up of many of the leading luminaries from the world of international arbitration. The committee includes the likes of John Beechey, Nish Shetty and Justin D'Agostino. There are two key objectives:

- to improve the profile and representation of women in arbitration; and
- to appoint women as arbitrators on an equal opportunity basis.

---

1   'Women and Power: Is The View Different?', Justice Sandra Day O'Connor, keynote speech at Washington University, November 1990.

While this in itself is very encouraging, an article in *Global Arbitration Review* in 2017[2] noted that Jacomijn van Haersolte-van Hof, the London Court of International Arbitration's director general, who had recently spoken at GAR London Live, had recorded her disappointment that: "arbitral institutions are doing the bulk of the work on promoting diversity rather than the parties or law firms".

At the same event, Richard Hill of Shell International was placing the blame firmly on the law firms, stating that his corporation "has no gender preference for arbitrators. Shell's own legal team is two thirds female owing to the number of women lawyers who move in house". While this last point is very heartening for Shell, and indeed in-house lawyers, I do wonder whether it is as encouraging for those who work in private practice. Is this a result of a wider problem for the women who initially commence their careers in private practice?

The article references an online discussion forum where a good degree of controversy was caused when the senior associate of a leading law firm suggested that the promise required by the pledge:

raises questions of how such firms are to balance their duty and their commitments under the pledge… Parties want to select the most well-known arbitrators. They were interested in winning their case – not changing the world.

The commentator was also quoted as saying:

Outside counsel's duty is to appoint an arbitrator in the best interests of the client, not necessarily in the best interests of diversity.

In the commercial arena, as suggested by Richard Hill, we have seen a growth in the number of women moving in house. This is also evidenced across the pond in the recent piece in *Big Law Business*,[3] which noted that "more and more women are being hired for the top lawyer jobs in Fortune 500 companies". Women in the position of general counsel now account for approximately 25% of the general counsel at Fortune 500 companies.

Returning to the Bar, I have read many reports and articles during my research for this chapter. There is much evidence to suggest that there is now parity in the number of women entering the profession, but it is equally clear that there is still a marked disparity between the numbers of women – compared to men – in silk and also in the senior ranks of the judiciary. While I will review some of the causes behind the gender gap in this chapter, I do not believe that I will reveal any new reasoning for it – the reasons have lived with us for rather a long time. Rather, I will focus on how things have changed, or not (paying particular attention to the last 20 years during which time I have been a senior clerk or equivalent).

During my time in chambers I have clerked near to 200 members of the Bar. When I started as a junior clerk in 1982 there were very few women practising. In fact, there were only two women in my first chambers. I arrived at my second chambers a year later to find none at all. The first joined a year later. There were no women silks in either. This was not an uncommon picture across the Bar at that time. In fact my research shows that only 20 women had been appointed silk by 1982. The

2   Alison Ross, 'A Year of the Pledge', *Global Arbitration Review*, 16 May 2017.
3   Stephanie Russell-Kraft, 'The Ranks of Women GCs are Growing', *Big Law Business*, June 2017.

respective clerks' rooms during my early years were also male dominated and at a senior level women were particularly thin on the ground. Of the leading chambers identified below, only two – 4 New Square (2 Crown Office Row as they then were) and Doughty Street Chambers – had women as senior clerks.

By the time that I was made senior clerk in 1997 both of my previous chambers had increased the number of women practitioners to five. But still none of them were in silk. However, the total numbers of women appointed silk by 1997 had now increased to 86; a growth of 330% in 15 years. When you consider that the numbers of men and women called to the Bar today are now equal, it would appear on first view that the gender diversity situation had significantly improved. However, there remains a significant gap across the Bar, particularly at the Commercial Bar. My former chambers (39 Essex Chambers) has 129 members, of whom 44 are women. The silk split is 42 men and eight women. The joint head of chambers is a woman and the management board consists of 12 members, six of whom are women. Again this looks encouraging progress, but what does a snapshot of the other sets look like?

The tables below include the records of a number of the leading chambers (in my opinion), of which there are 21, as listed in the 1998 and 2018 editions of Chambers and Partners' *Guide to the Legal Profession*.

Silks	2017			1997		
Chambers	Silks	Women	%	Silks	Women	%
One Crown Office Row	27	7	25.92	11	1	9.09
Doughty Street Chambers	35	9	25.71	11	1	9.09
Keating Chambers	29	7	24.13	10	0	0
Atkin Chambers	17	4	23.52	8	0	0
Monckton Chambers	14	3	21.42	7	0	0
Brick Court Chambers	38	8	21.05	22	1	4.54
39 Essex Chambers	42	8	19.04	11	0	0
4 New Square	25	4	16.00	7	0	0
Wilberforce Chambers	32	5	15.62	10	0	0

continued on next page

Silks	2017			1997		
Chambers	Silks	Women	%	Silks	Women	%
Blackstone Chambers	47	7	14.89	20	1	5
11 KBW	17	2	11.76	8	1	12.50
One Essex Court	35	4	11.42	20	1	5
Maitland Chambers	30	3	10.00	8	2	25
Landmark Chambers	31	3	9.67	12	0	0
8 New Square	12	1	8.33	8	1	12.5
Fountain Court Chambers	34	2	5.88	15	0	0
20 Essex Street	20	1	5.00	12	0	0
Quadrant Chambers	21	1	4.76	6	1	16.66
Serle Court Chambers	23	1	4.37	4	0	0
3 Verulam Buildings	23	1	4.34	11	1	9.09
Essex Court Chambers	47	2	4.25	16	0	0

Chambers name	Head of Chambers 1998–1999	Head of Chambers 2017	Total no of tenants 1998–1999	No of women tenants 1998–1999	Total no of tenants 2017	No of women tenants 2017
Blackstone Chambers	Presiley Baxendale QC and Charles Flint QC	Monica Carss-Frisk QC and Anthony Peto QC	54	14	103	26
39 Essex Chambers	Edwin Glasgow QC	Neil Block QC and Alison Foster QC	39	4	129	45
Brick Court Chambers	Christopher Clarke QC	Jonathan Hirst QC and Helen Davies QC	53	5	83	20
Fountain Court Chambers	Peter Scott QC	Stephen Moriarty QC	47	5	79	16
One Essex Court	Anthony Grabiner QC	Lord Grabiner QC	56	8	96	19
Landmark Chambers (previously 4 Breams Buildings)	Christopher Lockhart-Mummery QC	Richard Drabble QC and Neil Cameron QC	36	6	85	17
One Crown Office Row (previously 1 Crown Office Row)	Robert Seabrook QC	Philip Havers QC	42	8	73	24
4 New Square (previously 2 Crown Office Row)	John Powell QC	Mark Cannon QC	39	10	80	16
Essex Court Chambers	Gordon Pollock QC	Richard Jacobs QC and Graham Dunning QC	58	8	85	13
20 Essex Street	David Johnson QC	Christopher Hancock QC and Duncan Matthews QC	35	4	67	15
Monckton Chambers	Richard Fowler QC	Tim Ward QC and Philip Moser QC	24	5	61	14

continued on next page

Chambers name	Head of Chambers 1998–1999	Head of Chambers 2017	Total no of tenants 1998–1999	No of women tenants 1998–1999	Total no of tenants 2017	No of women tenants 2017
Doughty Street Chambers	Geoffrey Robertson QC	Geoffrey Robertson QC and Edward Fitzgerald CBE QC	48	13	133	55
11 King's Bench Walk	Eldred Tabachnik QC and James Goudie QC	James Goudie QC and John Cavanagh QC	30	4	61	16
Maitland Chambers (previously 13 Old Square)	Michael Lyndon-Stanford QC	Christopher Pymont QC	26	5	71	13
3 Verulam Buildings	R Neville Thomas QC	Ali Malek QC and Ewan McQuarter QC	48	11	68	14
Wilberforce Chambers	Edward Nugee QC	Michael Furness QC	29	6	68	15
8 New Square	Michael Fysh QC	Mark Platts-Mills QC	20	4	29	8
Atkin Chambers	John Blackburn QC	Andrew White QC	28	5	44	13
Keating Chambers	Richard Fernyhough QC	Marcus Taverner QC	32	5	58	15
Serle Court Chambers	Charles Sparrow QC	Alan Boyle QC	30	6	60	14
Quadrant Chambers (previously 4 Essex Court)	Nigel Teare QC	Luke Parsons QC	30	3	65	11

There were a number of notable facts. In 1997 the collective number of barristers in the above chambers totalled 804, of whom 139 were women (17.28%). Of those 139 women, 11 were in silk (7.9%). The total number of men in silk was 226 (35.9%).

In 1997 there were in fact only 86 women who had been appointed silk across the entire bar since 1949, when the first women silks, Helena Normanton and Rose Heilbron, were appointed, and only Blackstone Chambers had a woman as the head of chambers. In 2017 this number has increased to three.

By 2017 the selected chambers had a combined total of 1,598 barristers, of whom 399 were women (24.9%), leaving 1,199 men (75.1 %). There were 599 silks, of whom 83 were women and 516 were men. Women therefore only made up 13.8% of the total number of silks. While this is progress, it is not that much progress when you consider it is over a 20-year period.

The total number of women appointed silk across the entire bar as of 2017 has now reached 399. This represents an increase in numbers of 313 (364%) since 1997.

Let us return to 1997 and, more specifically, the (Student Special) Edition of *Legal Business*,[4] which focused on barristers under 40 at the junior bar. It will come as no surprise – given the statistics above – that at this time only three women were listed.

The three women listed were:

Helen Davies – Age 28 – Brick Court Chambers

Helen was described as "The best kept secret at the commercial bar? Not for long. Davies has all the makings of a future superstar."

Ten years after the publication of *Legal Business*'s list, Helen Davies was appointed silk. Today she is a hugely successful commercial silk and the joint head of chambers at Brick Court Chambers.

Finola O'Farrell – Age 36 – Keating Chambers

Her tenacious and clear-thinking style make O'Farrell a great favourite with leaders and solicitors alike. Living proof that you don't have to be an Oxbridge male to succeed at the Bar. Legal Business 1998 – "40 under 40"

In 2002 Finola was appointed silk. She had a stellar practice in construction law, a practice area which many would describe as particularly challenging for women. In 2016 she was appointed to the High Court Bench.

Mary Stokes – Age 39 – Erskine Chambers

A genuine academic. After her BCL at Brasenose College, Oxford, and a masters at Harvard (on the Kennedy Scholarship), Stokes went back to Brasenose to become a fellow and tutor in law for six years. Legal Business 1998 – "40 under 40"

Mary Stokes continues to practise at Erskine Chambers while also being a visiting professor in practice in the Department of Law at LSE. Chambers and Partners describe her as "a supreme company barrister, who is an intellectual giant and a joy to deal with".

The fact that in 1997 only three women had made the list was shocking. The author was equally outraged and went on to say:

Just three women made it into the 40. This is not the place to attempt to explain this shameful situation: suffice to say that it is high time the Bar admits it is still a male bastion and does something about it.

Interestingly – or perhaps worryingly – in 2017 *Legal Week*[5] listed its junior "stars at the bar". The slightly misleading accompanying photo has Andrew Lodder ranked by Lucy Cotton and Angeline Welsh, which would suggest that the list is female heavy. In actual fact, of the 12 barristers identified (and this includes the highly

---

4   *Legal Business Student Edition*, 1997.
5   'Stars at the Bar 2017 Revealed', *Legal Week*, Ben Rigby, 14 August 2017.

commended), the list – compiled from interviews with roughly 200 solicitors, barristers, Queen's Counsel and senior clerks – includes only three women. Of those, Angeline Welsh spent 14 years at Allen and Overy before switching to the Bar in 2015, which means that despite her exceptional achievements, the list includes only two established female practitioners.

However, the gender issue has been at the forefront of minds, of the industry bodies and in the media – as well as on a more individual level. On 1 September 2012 the Equality Rules of the Bar Standards Board Handbook[6] came into effect. The rules apply to self-employed barristers in multi-tenant chambers and include requirements to:

- produce an equality policy and action plan;
- appoint an equality and diversity officer and a diversity data officer;
- ensure chambers' selection panels are trained in fair recruitment;
- conduct diversity monitoring and analyse the data; and
- produce anti-harassment, flexible working, parental leave and reasonable adjustment policies.

This was moved on four years later by the Bar Standards Board 'Women at the Bar' report,[7] published in July 2016, which aimed to:

improve the BSB's knowledge of the implementation and effectiveness of the Equality Rules and to explore issues which may be contributing towards a lack of retention of female barristers.

The survey results showed a number of positives among those who responded, namely that there was high awareness of flexible working policies; recruitment was seen to be fair; the vast majority of chambers have equality policies in place; and awareness of maternity/parental leave is high. That said, it also highlighted a number of unresolved issues, including:

- many believe work allocation monitoring appears low, with lack of transparency the main issue;
- experiences of flexible working are mixed – for some it works well but others believe it has had a negative effect on their practice, such as an impact on work allocation or progression;
- many think that maternity/parental leave had a negative impact on their practice, with impacts on work allocation, progression and income highlighted. Responses also highlighted negative attitudes towards those returning from maternity leave as hindering a successful return to practice;
- two in every five said they had suffered harassment at the Bar, but only half had reported it. The most common reason for not reporting was concern for the impact on their career, with prevailing attitudes at the Bar towards harassment also a common reason;
- there were similar responses to discrimination, with two in every five saying they had experienced it. Here, discrimination from the clerks or in the allocation of work were more generally seen as prevalent; and

---

6   The Equality Rules of the Bar Standards Board Handbook, 1 December 2017.
7   Bar Standards Board 'Women at the Bar', July 2016.

- in terms of retention, most do not feel the rules (as per the handbook in 2012) have as yet had a significant impact in terms of supporting their careers. A large majority of respondents had also contemplated leaving the Bar.

A key question for me, based on my own experiences, and cemented by the results of the survey, is whether a barrister can combine the role of successful lawyer with that of a fulfilled home life. The expense of owning your own home or running a family household continues to grow at pace. This increasingly means that households often need both partners to be working, with the result being that it is ever-more difficult for barristers to combine their practice with family responsibilities.

I read an interesting report entitled 'Balanced Lives: Changing the Culture of Legal Practice', which was published by the American Bar Association in 2001. The report tackled the issues faced when attempting to find the balance between work and family life. The issues addressed were not gender specific; however, it contained this interesting reference:

> Leila Robinson was the first woman admitted to the Massachusetts State Bar. She put the following questions to an organisation of women lawyers and law students: "Is it practicable for a woman to successfully fulfil the duties of wife, mother and lawyer at the same time?" At the turn of the century, when the American Bar Association asked the same question, about a third of the female lawyers surveyed doubted that it was realistic to successfully combine the roles.[8]

This led me to wonder how a chambers' pupillage or tenancy committee would react to a candidate who embarks upon a discussion about his or her desire to live a balanced life in practice. My conclusion is that in all likelihood most interview panels will expect a woman to want to balance her practice with her family life and therefore would not have too much of an issue. However, would the same expectation apply for men? I suspect not. There is undoubtedly a growing desire among some men to share the demands of home and family life. Increasingly men are requesting paternity leave – something that was almost unheard of when I was a young clerk. One might say that if the progress made by women at the Bar was reflected in the same level of success of men in the home, then we might be making some serious headway. But even if the stereotypes are broken, or shall we say fractured, I doubt that an interview panel would react well to this sort of discussion at a pupillage interview.

In today's world legal competence is not sufficient on its own. There continues to be an expectation that barristers will do whatever is necessary to build and maintain a successful practice. Accessibility is perceived as critical and increasingly businesses are thought to expect a quick response from their lawyers. The advances in technology have only added to this, meaning that barristers can essentially always be 'on call' and drafted in for work of an urgent nature. Therefore longer hours have

8   Deborah L Rhode, 'Balanced Lives: Changing the Culture of Legal Practice', the American Bar Association, 2001.

to be worked to accommodate the clients' needs. Technology had not taken control when I started as a clerk. The pace of practice at that time, in many ways, suited the practitioner who wished to balance career and family life. Now, with technology moving at pace, there are many more women practising at the Bar. The irony is that the demands of modern technology have, in my view, actually made the environment for women at the Bar even more challenging. Technology was supposed to set us free but it has, in many ways, enslaved us in a world which expects 24/7 working. This enslavement is a problem that many of us face – it is clearly not a gender-specific issue. Men and women have to make career choices. The gender stereotypes in society are that men put their careers first while women put their families first. The challenge for society is whether this can be changed. Men and women at the Bar should have the freedom to choose the balanced life that works for them.

Admittedly, part of the problem is that barristers are usually unable to set their own deadlines. More often their deadlines are imposed by a judge or they are a result of their clients' perceived urgent needs. The unpredictable timing of the delivery of their instructions is also problematic. This, it should be noted, is not necessarily the fault of their lawyers or clients. It is, however, the result of a system which has become time critical. Barristers no longer have the luxury of being able to programme their work weeks in advance, something which in the past allowed them much more time to properly consider the issues before them. This expectation often leads to a collision between the competing demands of family and professional life.

The Bar, like many other industries, now finds itself in a situation where the work volumes have not kept pace with the supply of barristers. The leading chambers want to have a stable of the best barristers so as to maintain a significant market share of the work and ultimately a competitive advantage over their competitor sets.

There are more silks than ever competing in a highly competitive market. As we have seen, the vast majority of silks are men. However, most silks – whether men or women – are in high demand and command a high workload. As a result, great expectations of delivery are placed on their juniors. A busy commercial silk will inevitably require his or her juniors to work long hours and late shifts where necessary. Barristers are frequently interrupted whilst on their summer holiday – one of few that most take in a year – on the apparent urgent requirements of a case. The junior Bar, in particular, has never had to compete as it does today to secure a regular diet of advocacy. This can equally be said in respect of young juniors as well as more senior juniors. The general requirement to 'be available' has never been greater, mixed with the fact that competition for clients has never been as high.

I often ask myself whether clients really expect immediate availability. The overriding goal for them must surely be considered advice which helps them to make their business-critical decisions. However, the desire to offer exclusive availability can become a default when pitching for work; in my opinion, this should be the exception and not the rule. A cultural shift is required.

Barristers' clerks need to engage with their barristers so that they can manage, and sell, every individual's choice. Clerks have a role here as they should be empowering their barristers to take advantage of the flexibility that self-employment brings, allowing every member to make the right choice for them. They have a further important role in attempting to change client perceptions. As I said earlier, I am aware that this is not a problem just for the Bar; it sits with society as a whole.

This is where the role of the clerk is key. As a senior clerk it is imperative that you recognise the needs and wants of your barristers. These needs also, of course, have to be balanced with the requirements of the clients. Clerks need to ensure that teams are properly resourced so that the barristers can provide an effective service. Clients do not benefit from exhausted barristers and the pressure for one person to do the work of two should be resisted.

In many ways I think it is too easy to put a 'woman' label on this issue. There have been many changes at the Bar over the last 20 years. The structures are now in place to facilitate choice. However, for these structures to properly succeed, society has to change the way in which it differentiates between men and women.

I recall clerking my first woman barrister. There was no maternity policy and she felt pressured to return to work quickly. Today we have flexible maternity/paternity policies, but the pressures to return remain as great as they were when I began my career.

The high-pressured nature of the work often leads to other problems. Stress and mental health issues are increased by excessive workloads. That is even without taking into consideration the added pressures of family responsibilities.

There have been numerous well-intentioned initiatives instigated by the Bar Council to raise awareness of these issues and help with the challenge of balancing a family life with a barrister's professional practice. One of the initiatives was the Bar Nursery programme which was launched by the Bar Council in 2013. However, the idea of the Bar Nursery Scheme became a battleground as members of the professions fought to secure a suitable space within the Inns of Court. After five years of negotiation the Bar Nursery was launched outside the Inns of Court. The nursery is open between 7am and 7pm, with the long opening hours designed to assist those whose practice involves extensive travel to appear in courts all over the country. Maura McGowan (now Dame Maura McGowan), chairman of the Bar Council at the time, said in a press statement:

> The Bar Council is committed to supporting parents and ensuring that the profession retains its best people. Owing to the nature of work at the Bar, many parents find it exceptionally difficult to juggle childcare responsibilities with their ever-changing work schedule, particularly those barristers who regularly appear in court, which can mean travelling to different towns every day. It is important that members of the profession are not discouraged from starting a family because of their work, which could have a detrimental effect particularly on the number of women choosing a career at the Bar, and could see talented practitioners leaving the self-employed Bar for a more stable working life in employed practice, or even another profession.[9]

Interestingly, the original plan was to open somewhere within the Inns of Court, but the idea was rejected by the Inns themselves. As a result the nursery was finally opened in partnership with Smithfield House Nursery.

---

9   'Bar Council launches first ever Bar Nursery', The Bar Council, 16 April 2013.

As I addressed at the start of this chapter, I recognise that gender diversity is not just a problem at the Bar, but for the whole legal market – both domestically and internationally.

A lack of gender balance in the judiciary is also a topic frequently debated. Earlier this year, there was cause for celebration when Baroness Hale was appointed President of the Supreme Court. She is the first woman Lord of Appeal in Ordinary after a varied career as an academic lawyer, law reformer and judge. In October 2009 she became the first woman justice of the Supreme Court.

In July 2017 the appointment of The Rt Hon Lady Justice Black DBE was approved by the Queen, meaning that when her appointment takes effect there will be two women in the Supreme Court. With 11 Justices currently, this means that women will make up 18% of the quota.

This might at first glance appear disappointing given that we are approaching 100 years since the Sex Disqualification (Removal) Act in 1919. However, if one reflects on where we were 20 years ago, then the progression is significant. The important issue is to keep up the momentum.

In 2017 history was made in New Zealand when Chief Justice Dame Sian Elias, the first woman to hold the office of Chief Justice, was joined by Justice Susan Glazebrook and Justice Ellen France. They, together with Justices William Young and Mark O'Regan, made up New Zealand's Supreme Court Bench for a case concerning an appeal relating to alleged discrimination affecting airline pilots. For the first time, there were more women than men on the Supreme Court Bench.

Chris Moore, who heads the New Zealand Law Society's women's advisory group, was quoted in an article on the Radio New Zealand website at the time, saying that 68% of the judiciary were men and it was important the law profession fixed its gender diversity issues, especially around women returning to the workforce after having children:

> Frankly if we don't do that we will have women leaving the profession and we simply can't afford to lose that talent, so we need to be more flexible in the way we practice and we need to look at a lot of the unconscious bias areas where so many of us fall into traps.[10]

He pointed out that, despite this, New Zealand was doing much better than the United Kingdom. He also highlighted the progress in Australia, where three out of seven judges in its highest court are women and Canada, where women make up four out of nine of their Supreme Court judges.

The Judicial Diversity Statistics, published by the Ministry of Justice in July 2017, show that currently 28% of court judges and 45% of tribunal judges are women. Fifty-four per cent of magistrates are women.

The report showed that among court judges, senior roles had a lower representation of women judges than those in less senior roles. This was less evident among tribunal judges, with a more equal representation of women at all levels of tribunal appointments.

---

10   Annie Marie May, 'History-making majority-female Supreme Court bench', Radio New Zealand website, 13 June 2017.

Around half of all court judges and just under two-thirds of tribunal judges aged under 40 are female.

The chart below, taken from the Judicial Diversity Report 2017, shows female representation at each court judge role as of 1 April 2017:

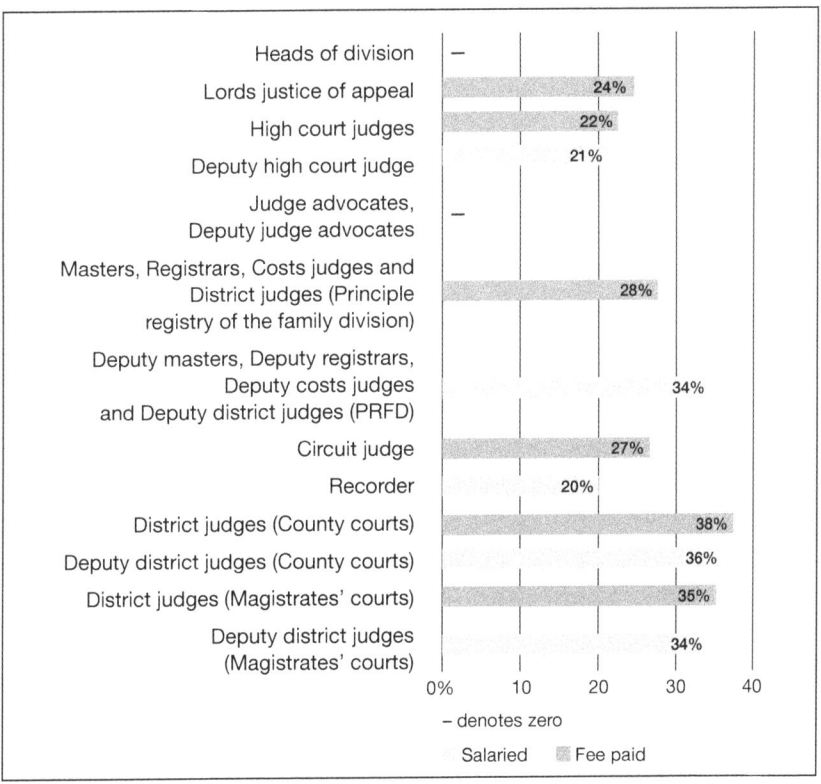

Source: Judicial Diversity Report 2017 © Crown Copyright

It is clear that achieving diversity within the judiciary has not been as fast as one might hope. As Baroness Hale said in a speech in August 2017:

It is a priority to achieve better representation of half of the human race on the bench. Judging should be informed as much by the experience of leading a woman's life as it is by the experience of leading a man's.[11]

Despite the slow pace, the commitment to accelerating it must be noted. The Judicial Diversity Committee was formed in 2013. It is chaired by Lady Justice Hallett and has, each year, pursued more initiatives to explore what might be done to speed up the process. It is widely supported by judges across England and Wales and, in April 2017, the committee published a progress report and action plan for the next 12 months.

---

11 'Judges, Power and Accountability, Constitutional Implications of Judicial Selection', Lady Hale speech at the Constitutional Law Summer School, Belfast, 11 August 2017.

However, if I were to conclude that the fact that the weight of numbers of women lawyers entering the profession will eventually result in gender equality across the profession within the next few years, then sadly I think that I would be mistaken.

The very limited increase in silk appointments between 1997 and the present day suggests that progress is incredibly slow. In fact, if we were to extrapolate the figures then we are unlikely to achieve gender equality of silks until 2078. As *Legal Business* put it, this would be shameful. One would certainly have expected the progress to present differently given the number of women that have entered the profession in the last 20 years.

Women must be given a fair opportunity to develop the practice of their choosing with a fair allocation of unassigned work. Ultimately it is about choice and opportunity. Choice is straightforward. Opportunity presents a much greater issue. My research suggests that due to stereotypes women are not always given access to the work of their choosing. An article in *Counsel Magazine* (February 2017) lent a degree of criticism towards clerks for leading women barristers' practices in a particular direction for reasons associated with gender as opposed to ability. This practice clearly has the potential to prejudice a woman's chance of satisfying the criteria when making a silk application.

Some might suggest that many women do not wish to pursue silk or judicial office due to family responsibilities. I would argue against this notion. Women, and increasingly men, need to devote time to their families. The key issue is for clerks to properly engage with their barristers to agree a plan for their practice which includes the provision of career breaks for those that wish to take them.

The Bar Council has done much to facilitate a number of initiatives to support women and encourage chambers to address the issue of gender equality in the profession. However, unless there is a cultural change in chambers, the initiatives will only ever have limited success.

I have been privy to conversations between senior women barristers suggesting mentoring of young women barristers by other, more senior women. I personally do not agree with this as a concept. It should be senior barristers mentoring junior barristers, regardless of gender. Given that there continues to be a large disparity of men and women silks, it follows that a gender-specific mentoring programme would only serve to disadvantage women.

During my research period, I attended a 'First 100 Years' event. The event is part of a history project, supported by the Law Society and Bar Council, charting the journey of women in law since 1919. I think there were, at most, two men in attendance and in excess of 100 women, highlighting the fact that men do not attend women-focused events.

I therefore wonder whether women networks – on their own – will help to advance the issue of gender equality. In my view, the lack of engagement by men in these types of event means that, while worthwhile, much more needs to be done to complement them by addressing the cultural issues that still exist in many chambers.

Another issue I have encountered as a clerk is the stereotyping of female as opposed to male characteristics. New Zealand's Justice Susan Glazebrook wrote an interesting paper in the December 2013 issue of *At the Bar*, which addressed issues similar to those discussed in this chapter.

She wrote:

In the 1970s there were around 10% female members of US orchestras. This had increased to 35% in the mid-1990s. Why the increase? The acquisition of "larger techniques" by women musicians you venture? Not at all – the increase has been attributed to the introductions of musicians auditioning behind a screen so that the gender of the players was unknown. This story shows that our perceptions of merit can be influenced by our subconscious biases.[12]

This continues to be discrimination when it comes to the perceived characteristics of women and men. Mrs Justice Glazebrook also addressed the issue which resonated with me as a clerk. She referenced the findings of two psychologists who, in 2007, undertook research on gender discrimination and other challenges faced by professional women.[13] Alice Eagly and Linda Carli's research found that people associate men and women with different traits and link men with more traits that connote leadership (at least the old-fashioned view of leadership). Women are associated with communal qualities, which convey a concern for the compassionate treatment of others. By contrast, men are associated with qualities such as assertion and control.

There is still a long way to go to change these perceptions. Mrs Justice Glazebrook's paper directed me to Avivah Wittenburg-Cox's four-part strategy for achieving gender balance.[14] First, carry out a 'gender audit' to assess the gender balance and compare it to your competitors. Second, the 'awareness phase' involves bringing home the importance of gender balance issues to the management of chambers. Third, the 'alignment phase', where awareness is translated into the process systems of your organisation. The final stage is 'sustainability'. True change can take decades to achieve, so the impetus must be maintained.

If those responsible for implementing change within chambers can properly engage with the gender diversity issue, then they may have some chance of achieving some significant changes.

However, let me not leave it here. On a positive note, women are succeeding in the legal profession in greater numbers every year, highlighted not least in the past year by the appointment of Baroness Hale as the first female President of the Supreme Court and Liz Truss as the first female Lord Chancellor. It was also recently reported in the *Evening Standard*[15] that a judge at Southwark Crown Court has ordered that women barristers must be given access to 'Rumpolian' all-male locker rooms used by lawyers during major trials. The move came after female advocates said they were excluded from crucial conversations about cases, and the space will now be unisex and open to men and women QCs and their legal teams. Judge Deborah

---

12   Hon Justice Susan Glazebrook, 'It is Just a Matter of Time and Other Myths', *At the Bar*, December 2013.
13   Alice Eagly and Linda L Carli, 'Women and the Labyrinth of Leadership', *Harvard Business Review*, September 2007.
14   Avivah Wittenberg-Cox, 'How Women Mean Business: A Step by Step Guide to Profiting from Gender Balanced Business', May 2010.
15   Jonathan Prynn, 'Female barristers win right to use all-male locker room at London court', *Evening Standard*, 21 August 2017.

Taylor who ruled on the change stated, quite rightly, that "gender should play no part in the role or status of a barrister".

It is clear that much progress has been made but we need to do more, much more, in order to maintain momentum. Without a cultural change, I fear that the policies and recommendations merely pay lip service to a problem that should have been left behind many years ago. Diversity is an asset and should be embraced in order that we are much closer to gender equality come the end of the next decade, as opposed to the next century.

The author would like to thank Beth Williams of 39 Essex Chambers for her assistance in the compilation of this chapter.

Wellbeing

Nicholas Hill
3 New Square IP

1. Introduction

Amidst the many changes that have taken place at the Bar over recent years, one particularly stands out: the discussion and implementation of support around issues of wellbeing. Why should that be noteworthy? After all, wellbeing and mindfulness are topics that are now firmly in the public arena, so why should the Bar be any different? The aim of this chapter is to provide an introduction to the topic of wellbeing and information on what sets, individual barristers and chambers personnel can do to assist their members and staff in remaining productive and healthy.

As we will go on to see, there is a risk that a career at the Bar, combined with the characteristics often held by those who are barristers, can create a 'perfect storm' of conditions in which wellbeing and mental health issues can develop. The Bar is a competitive arena, barristers as individuals are competitive, and even at a high-level view, one can see that a high-performing individual – a sole practitioner, self-reliant, often working alone and under pressure – may be at risk of issues such as rumination and perfectionism which, left unchecked, can result in mental health issues.

2. What is wellbeing?

'Wellbeing' will mean different things to different people and will vary from setting to setting. In the context of the Bar, and the Wellbeing at the Bar (WATB) project, the following definition is used: "Wellbeing is about having the resilience and ability to carry out your professional duties in a healthy way."

3. Why is it important?

While it may now be accepted that the Bar is an environment which can give rise to mental health issues, for many years wellbeing and mental health were rarely spoken about. The competitiveness that exists at the Bar meant that many felt that disclosing a mental health or wellbeing issue was akin to a sign of weakness. There were fears that if 'the market' were to become aware that an individual suffered from a mental health issue, this would somehow indicate that he was unable to carry out his job and fewer instructions would therefore follow. The result was that individuals were often unable to ask for, or receive, the support they required.

Tackling the idea that a mental health condition is a sign of weakness is particularly important; successful barristers may be particularly at risk as they might have the characteristics, such as perfectionism, rumination or an ambitious focus to succeed, which can be causes of mental illness.

The business case for wellbeing support is well documented. By the time a barrister is in practice, he will have completed a pupillage, supported by a financial award from chambers. His colleagues in chambers will have supplemented this by their own time in providing training during pupillage. The set itself is likely to have introduced the barrister to its key clients, and once in practice, the barrister will have built up goodwill with these clients and will be earning fees in his own name as well as the possibility of introducing other barristers in chambers to those that he knows, increasing the potential pool of those being instructed.

Against this background, a barrister who is not performing due to a wellbeing issue will have a potential effect on a number of areas. If the barrister is unable to work for any period of time, the most obvious effect will be the reduction in earnings, both for the individual and, by extension, his chambers contribution. But there are other important areas too; an individual who is unwell and not performing can have a detrimental effect on colleagues and those with whom he is working. In a chambers environment where barristers may be working in teams, the effect can be more acute. It may also be felt by chambers' employees, resulting in an atmosphere that makes it difficult for clerks and other staff to perform at their best. In addition, there is a client element – both in a human sense and the attendant professional risk – in an individual working when not fully well.

It is important to remember that many organisations, including law firms, are investing in their understanding of and offering of support in mental health issues. The traditional view that there may be a detrimental result from informing clients that a barrister is encountering a wellbeing issue needs to be challenged from the modern angle, which is that the conversations that will take place in dealing with a wellbeing issue will be received with understanding and a desire that the outcome is a quick resolution to the individual's suffering and a swift return to work.

It is equally important that chambers' staff are supported in their own wellbeing and their dealings with those who may be unwell.

4. The science behind the issue

Much has been written about the science behind wellbeing. By way of simple explanation, every day an individual will encounter any number of situations. These situations will vary and will be experienced on various scales – for example, from good to bad, pleasant to unpleasant, relaxing to stressful etc. On every occasion the brain's neural circuits react by creating neural messages. These messages cause a change in the brain's chemistry, and it is this reaction that alters the brain's state of arousal, governing how we think, feel and behave. This state of arousal has a direct effect on an individual's performance.

It is the relationship between mental arousal and performance that was developed by the psychologists Robert Yerkes and John Dodson and resulted in the Yerkes-Dodson law. Their research showed that while mental arousal resulted in increased performance, there is a point at which arousal becomes too high and performance suffers as a result. This can be shown graphically on the following chart:

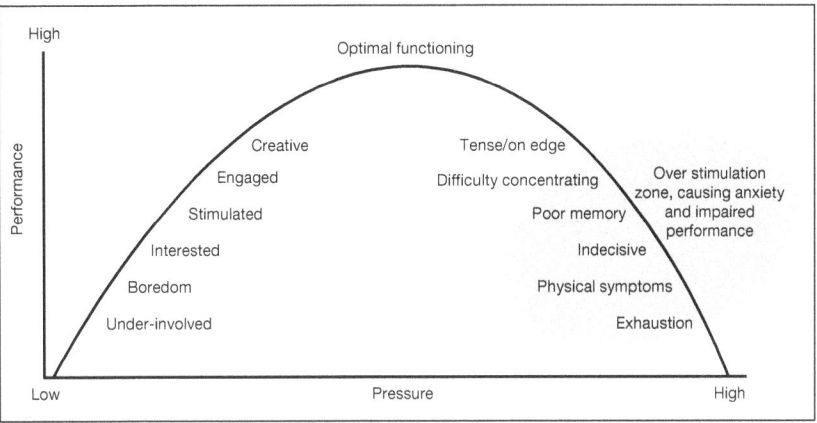

Source: Benedict Hill

As can be seen from the chart, one of the key matters to keep in mind when working with others to obtain their best is that optimal performance is achieved when there is pressure on the individual to perform. Indeed, for anyone to perform at his best a level of pressure is required. The point at the top of the curve is where performance reaches its optimal point. An individual can stay in this zone for a long time, but without a reduction in pressure, or with an increase in pressure, there is a risk that one moves from optimal functioning to the other side of the curve, where performance and efficiency are reduced and wellbeing is affected.

Thus, the chart shown can be developed further to show that to keep optimal performance requires a movement within the optimal zone where pressure is varied:

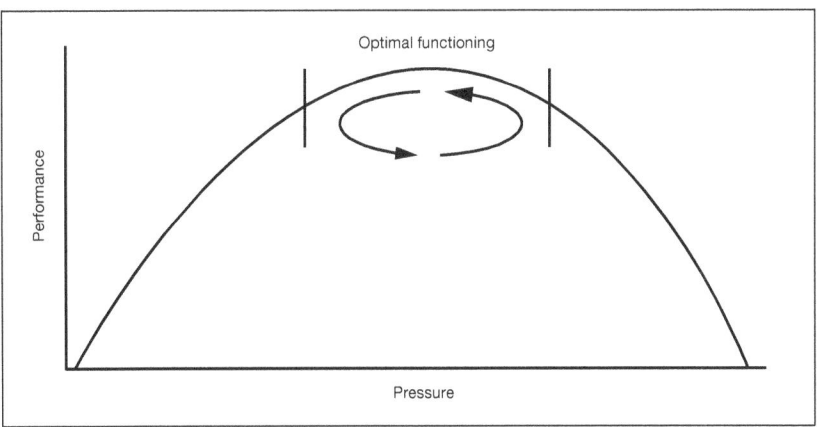

Source: Benedict Hill

Although this may on first appearance look complex, it can be easily summarised as follows: to allow an individual to work at his best, after periods of high pressure he will need release to move back to a less pressured position before returning again to a pressured state. This could be as simple as ensuring that a barrister has sufficient down time following a trial before he commences the next, or allowing a member of staff who has been working on a big project some time off after its completion.

It is where an individual sits on the curve that will determine his ability to perform, and that is why communication is of key importance in matters of wellbeing; it is through communication that we are able to understand where colleagues and ourselves are in terms of pressure, and thereby understand their and our mental capacity and ability to perform.

In addition, it should be noted that there will be a need for an individual to take time out of the optimal zone; this is why holidays are so important to mental wellbeing – they allow for a balance in life and an opportunity for self-care.

The pressures that affect performance are not solely those of the workplace; personal and other external factors will also play a part. The benefits of managing pressure are not to be found solely in the workplace – there is a strong correlation between emotional stability and resilience having a positive effect both on satisfaction in life and health as well as performance at work.

This applies to everyone, barristers and staff, across all practice areas.

5.   The Bar's journey to date – a brief history

Rachel Spearing, a barrister from Pump Court Chambers and former circuit junior of the Western Circuit, founded the Wellbeing at the Bar (WATB) working group in 2014. Together with Sam Mercer, head of equality & diversity and corporate social responsibility at the Bar Council, she led an initial working group of six bodies (the Bar Council, the four Inns of Court and the Institute of Barristers' Clerks) with the aim of developing a programme that would provide barristers and clerks with the information and skills they needed to stay well; to support barristers and clerks as they dealt with wellbeing difficulties that affected their professional lives; and to provide assistance to those, or supporting those, in difficulty or crisis.

The first project, undertaken in late 2014, was a survey sent to all practising barristers that posed a number of evidence-based questions proven to test for levels of psychological health and performance. The survey was completed by 2,456 barristers across a wide range of seniorities and practice areas. The results were circulated in a report[1] in April 2015 and stated a number of key findings:

- 1 in 3 barristers found it difficult to control/stop worrying;
- 2 in 3 felt showing signs of stress equalled weakness;
- 1 in 6 felt in low spirits most of the time;
- 59% demonstrated unhealthy levels of perfectionism; and
- psychological wellbeing within the profession was rarely spoken about.

It was against this background that the working group was expanded to include all the specialist Bar associations, and focused primarily on developing an online web portal which would deliver information and support for all those in chambers by providing resources on staying well, recognising the signs of being unwell and ways to remedy them, and returning from being unwell to wellness.

---

1   www.barcouncil.org.uk/media/348371/wellbeing_at_the_bar_report_april_2015__final_.pdf

The result was the WATB website, which was launched at the Bar Conference in October 2016.[2] The site proved to be an immediate and valuable resource, and received nearly 80,000 hits in the first six months.

6. Wellbeing at the Bar web resource

When considering wellbeing for chambers, it is important to allow each set the flexibility to reflect its culture and ethos. While best practice would suggest that as part of supporting barristers and staff in matters of wellbeing a set should have a wellbeing policy, there is no 'one size fits all' solution.

We will go on to consider what may be included in a wellbeing policy, but first it is worth exploring in more detail the offering of the WATB website, because that provides much of the information that chambers or individual barristers may require.

6.1 Staying well

The starting point is providing the necessary information to stay well. As will be seen from above, there is an optimal functioning zone and many people are able to stay and work in this zone for long periods of time. However, the move out of the optimal functioning zone is not dependent on how long someone has remained within it. The move out can be rapid, even if the time within the zone has lasted for many years.

The web resource is particularly helpful in this way because it acknowledges the particular pressures that are experienced by members of the Bar and those working with them: working hours, the peaks and troughs of work levels, demands of email and dealing with difficult people. Adding to this the demands of personal lives and commitments, one can see the ability for an individual to become overloaded, for pressure to increase, and for the individual to move to the wrong side of the Yerkes-Dodson curve.

This is explained by an excellent short animation available on the website, written and narrated by Dr Bill Mitchell, under the 'Staying Well' heading.[3]

The section continues to provide information on the five drivers of personal wellbeing as identified by the New Economics Foundation, namely:

- taking notice of thoughts and feelings;
- the benefits of regular physical activity;
- the benefits of social contact and the harm of being isolated;
- the benefits of learning; and
- the benefits of giving, including of time.

6.2 Supporting colleagues and recognising the signs

If we have identified that to remain well one needs to be working within the optimal zone, it is important to be able to recognise when an individual or colleague is moving out of the zone. When considering these cases it should be remembered that

---

2   www.wellbeingatthebar.org.uk.
3   www.wellbeingatthebar.org.uk/staying-well/.

a one-off situation, such as shortness of temper or worry, does not necessarily mean that an individual is entering a stressed zone. However, if changes are observed over a few weeks, this may be an indication that the person concerned may need assistance.

These signs can be broken down into the following three areas

(a)   *Psychological*

These are the internal, mental patterns that arise from being stressed, and common indicators include anxiety, depression, loss of confidence, loss of humour, inability to focus, sense of dread or inability to make a decision.

(b)   *Physiological*

These are the experiences we notice in our bodies when we are under stress, and include excessive tiredness or insomnia, headaches, aching muscles, high blood pressure or stomach complaints.

(c)   *Behavioural*

These are the outward expressions of a stress reaction, and include excessive drinking, substance abuse, over or under eating, insomnia, poor memory, avoidance, confusion, obsessive behaviour or inability to concentrate.

These lists are not exhaustive and there will be other examples in each category, but all three behaviours may be observed in ourselves or in others. By knowing the signs it is possible to consider what action may be required and to consider whether, and how, to intervene.

6.3   Helping colleagues: having a wellbeing conversation

The process of joining a set of chambers and the workings of the chambers model mean that barristers and staff often work together as colleagues for many years. This has a particular benefit in the field of wellbeing as it is the knowledge of colleagues over long periods of time that might make it more likely to recognise a change in behaviour.

It is worth remembering, however, that wellbeing is an area in which there still remains some stigma, and that although there has been great progress in breaking this down, it does mean that some of those who are unwell will be reluctant to raise it as an issue. Equally, they may exhibit few of the signs detailed. Further, as reported on the WATB website, as human beings we are adept at masking concerns or worries and so the need for intervention may not be obvious. This highlights again why working to break down the stigma and develop a culture of openness in relation to wellbeing is so important. If support is to be given to those who are unwell, there needs to be a culture in which they feel able to ask for help; if they cannot raise it their friends and colleagues will not be able to assist in helping to resolve the issue. Encouraging open communication will allow someone who is unwell to acknowledge and communicate that to others, diluting the expectation on colleagues and friends to know instinctively if someone is unwell.

One of the largest hurdles in dealing with a wellbeing issue is for the person who is unwell simply to talk about it. The acknowledgement that someone is unwell or that they require help means that a healing process can begin. Therefore, the need for, and how to have, a wellbeing conversation is of crucial importance. In some ways it does not matter who has the conversation, but there will obviously be factors to consider such as whether the conversation is to be barrister to barrister, clerk to clerk or barrister to clerk (or vice versa). The important thing is that the conversation takes place with a person who will listen to concerns, can be trusted and will be able to help address the issues raised. The WATB website is an excellent source of information for practical tips to help have such a conversation.[4]

7.   Policies for chambers

The progress made across the profession in breaking down the stigma attached to mental health and discussing wellbeing issues has meant that many chambers have started considering ways that they can support their members and staff and to improve the culture around wellbeing issues.

A key way in which this can be done is through the adoption of a wellbeing policy. A policy such as this will have a dual role: not only will it set out the basis on which the chambers approaches the subject, it will also give permission for those within the set to have conversations about wellbeing without the fear of stigma and improve the culture in this area.

Each set can tailor the policy that it will adopt; again, there is no one size fits all. For example, the ways in which a policy will operate will need to reflect the chambers' working; a large set specialising in crime where barristers are in court every day is likely to have different considerations to a set where paper and written work is most common.

There are a number of sources from which a policy can be taken. From its initial launch, the WATB website provided sample policies that could be adopted by chambers. Since then the Chancery Bar Association in conjunction with the Institute of Barristers' Clerks launched a Wellbeing Best Practice policy.[5]

In considering a policy, some of the headings in the Chancery Bar Association/ Institute of Barristers' Clerks policy may be helpful to those sets that prefer to draft their own. The policy should clearly set out the objectives and strategies; in this case four broad topics were covered:

- recognise the importance of, and raise awareness of the need for, a healthy lifestyle;
- improve wellbeing in chambers through two-way communication and an appropriate workload;
- improve relationships and encourage discussion of personal issues in order to improve wellbeing; and
- provide support for barristers and staff who may experience a wellbeing issue.

Another policy used by a large common law chambers has the following objectives:

---

4   www.wellbeingatthebar.org.uk/help-a-colleague/.
5   www.chba.org.uk/for-members/well-being/best-practice-policy.

- to develop a supportive culture, address factors that may negatively affect mental wellbeing and to develop management skills;
- to provide support for staff, pupils and barristers experiencing mental health difficulties; and
- to demonstrate a positive and enabling attitude to employees and job applicants with mental health issues.

The policy should set out the responsibilities for disseminating and implementing the policy and conclude with the commitment to review the policy at regular intervals and to amend or improve the policy based on experience.

An additional consideration for implementing such a policy is that it sets out an understanding for all members and staff should a wellbeing issue arise, as well as assisting those in chambers who will have to consider whether a wellbeing issue in chambers may have a regulation element.

8. Wellbeing and regulation

With the ever-increasing reach of regulation it is not surprising that issues of wellbeing also have the potential to fall within regulated conduct. As with other areas, the WATB website has a full section on what can be a tricky topic, which can be found under the 'Resources: Policy and Practice' heading, and much of the following information is taken from that resource.

There is a real tension here; chambers as organisations will wish to support a member of chambers who may be suffering from a wellbeing issue and also to comply with their requirements under the Bar Standards Board (BSB) Code as well as the law generally. Of course, anyone suffering from a wellbeing issue is likely already to have many concerns and the thought of notification or reporting to the BSB will only add to those concerns, putting additional pressure on the individual at a time when it is least welcome, and potentially putting the chambers in a double bind in its obligations to the individual and to the regulatory body.

There are four areas that may require consideration.

8.1 Serious misconduct

This may arise where a barrister suffering from a wellbeing issue may have directly or indirectly committed misconduct as a result of his condition. 'Misconduct' is defined as a breach of the obligations under the BSB handbook. Full information is contained in the WATB's 'Serious Misconduct Guidance'. Briefly, two main duties may arise:

- In some circumstances, there will be a duty to report the misconduct to the BSB.
- A barrister who commits misconduct is under a duty (flowing from Core Duties 2 and 10) to take all reasonable steps to mitigate the effects of that misconduct (gC2, gC94). A failure to comply with either of those duties will itself be misconduct. If you are working in an entity, then misconduct falling short of serious misconduct should be reported to your HOLP so that this can be recorded: see gC102.

However, as Andrew Walker QC, Chairman Ethics Committee (2016) and Bar Chair for 2018, has pointed out:

In general, we anticipate that the BSB is likely to take a proportionate approach, and be content for chambers to go as far as they sensibly and reasonably can and wish to go to manage a wellbeing issue internally, up to the point at which (1) this raises a risk to any duties under the Handbook, (2) the public interest is compromised, or (3) a significant risk of adverse consequences arises for clients, the public, the profession or members of chambers.[6]

8.2   Fitness to practice

This covers the situation where a barrister's ability to practise may be impaired by a physical or mental health condition. For it to be a consideration the barrister in question must have a current practising certificate and the health condition must also have an impact on the barrister's practice, rather than being a concern generally.

The full provisions of fitness to practice are contained in Section E of the BSB Handbook. Under the definition in the BSB Handbook, 'unfit to practice' means that a barrister is:

incapacitated due to his or her physical or mental condition (including any addiction); and, as a result, the Individual's fitness to practice is impaired and the imposition of a restriction; or the acceptance of undertakings in lieu, is necessary for the protection of the public, is otherwise in the public interest or is in the individual's own interests.

Fitness to practice procedures are less formal than a disciplinary tribunal and are held in private. The independent panel is concerned with the impact of any health condition upon the public, the public interest or on the barrister himself if there were no restrictions upon practice.

8.3   Discrimination and harassment

Consideration arising under this area is where chambers may be treating a barrister or member of staff unfairly because of his physical or mental health condition. As detailed in the Handbook at gC96.2, harassment and victimisation may amount to serious misconduct.

8.4   Other duties relevant to individuals and chambers

Consideration here covers situations where a barrister may be failing to run his practice appropriately, or to perform his role (or act towards others) appropriately within chambers, as a result of a physical or mental health condition. Although they are not dealt with specifically as issues arising from wellbeing, the following BSB Handbook provisions may be relevant in a wellbeing situation:

- Core duty CD10: You must take reasonable steps to manage your practice, or carry out your role within your practice, competently and in such a way as to achieve compliance with your legal and regulatory obligations.
- Equality and Diversity: rC110.3   You must take reasonable steps to ensure that in relation to your chambers or *BSB authorised body*, ... the following requirements are complied with:

---

6   www.wellbeingatthebar.org.uk/policy-and-practice/

        • If you are a *self-employed barrister*, the affairs of your *chambers* are conducted in a manner which is fair and equitable for all members of *chambers, pupils* and/or *employees* (as appropriate). This includes, but is not limited to, the fair distribution of work opportunities among *pupils* and members of *chambers*.

        Where mental or physical health is concerned, wider equality and diversity obligations may also be triggered.

- Chambers management: rC89 Taking into account the provisions of Rule C90, you must take reasonable steps to ensure that:

    .1 your *chambers* is [*sic*] administered competently and efficiently;

    .8 appropriate risk management procedures are in place and are being complied with.

The focus of those provisions is likely to be seen as being risks to clients, but wellbeing issues may in some situations give rise to such risks. The management of such risks, and any policies in that regard, are a matter for each set of chambers.

- Other chambers policies: If chambers has its own wellbeing or best practice policy in place, it should be consulted to check whether any obligations arise beyond those mentioned above.

9.   A case study

The following case study attempts to take many of the issues considered above and give a sense of how a wellbeing situation might arise and be rectified.

Barrister B is a junior barrister of seven years' call in a large multi-discipline set which offers expertise in a number of areas of civil law. B's own practice covers three different work areas, has a combination of cases both led and unled, and has a near half-and-half split of court work and paperwork. At the start of practice B's work was mostly as the junior being led on large cases, but in recent years B's reputation has increased, more work has been unled and the volume of cases offered has increased. B is ambitious and has wanted to accept cases in order to build up a broad contact list that will support B through the years of practice. A wellbeing situation arose when a number of factors came together at the same time.

First, B was instructed as the only junior in a large case being led by a Queen's Counsel. The case was demanding and was set for an expedited trial that required the junior to spend time working on evidence in a tight timescale. Although a Queen's Counsel was instructed, the silk in question did not have sufficient time to work properly on the case and much was left to B, including some large strategic questions.

Second was the offer of a case from a solicitor that B and the chambers had been targeting for some time and which B decided could be accommodated around other work.

Finally, during a particularly demanding period of time, B was informed that a close family member had been diagnosed with a terminal illness. It was this final piece of information that caused B real difficulty; it kept playing on B's mind and made it hard to concentrate. When demands came in from other sources B began to struggle with prioritising and questioned the demands of clients against the terminal illness of his relative.

This continued for some weeks and, in the way that was described in the Yerkes-Dodson illustration, B's work began to suffer as B moved into a high-pressured, but low-performance state. Although B did not show any signs at work, B's partner noticed that all was not right and suggested that B might consult a doctor. After a referral to a mental health specialist, it became clear that in order for B to recover a period of time away from work would be required.

B enjoyed a good working relation with clerk C, and was able to explain what had been happening over the last few weeks and that time away from work was going to be required. Chambers had a wellbeing policy and B and C worked out a planned series of meetings and actions that would allow for a period of leave but with planned return to work. B and C worked to three broad stages and agendas:

- Pre-leave meeting:
    - agree last working day;
    - any time required for medical appointments to be prioritised;
    - current cases review – agree re-allocation with instructing solicitors;
    - agree information to be given to solicitors/other enquiries;
    - set provisional return date;
    - review fees and aged debt to cover period of leave;
    - allocate mentor for period of leave;
    - logistics for period of leave: post, payments received, subscriptions etc; and
    - B and C catch up and review dates.

- During leave:
    - agree regular catch-up telephone calls/meetings;
    - review provisional return date;
    - mentoring requirements;
    - update on cases and enquiries received;
    - review of fees received; and
    - date for next meeting.

- Return to work meeting:
    - agree working days and hours;
    - agree workload parameters;
    - consider return to work notification to chambers and clients;
    - pre-leave cases – take back cases?;
    - agree contact with instructing solicitors for future work opportunities;
    - review fees received and aged debt; and
    - set date for full practice review.

10.   Conclusion

There is much more that can be said on the topic of wellbeing; the WATB website contains excellent further resources. It is clearly beneficial for chambers to create a culture where issues can be discussed openly and sensitively, and the implementation of a wellbeing policy is a good first step towards achieving that aim. With the information contained on the WATB website and highlighted in this chapter, sets of chambers now have the tools to develop their own policy and a positive approach to the issue of wellbeing.

Compliance and risk management

Christine Kings
Outer Temple Chambers

1. Introduction

The Bar survives on its reputation. Traditionally this has been about how well a barrister performs in court and the quality of service provided to the client. The positive reputation of a chambers is largely built on the quality of its barristers and the work of their clerking and administrative teams. Developing strong client relationships, building trust and attracting good casework are essential elements for success. Many chambers create brands and spend significant amounts of money on PR agencies and marketing staff. Respect in the profession comes from being excellent lawyers, recognition in the directories, and being a chambers noted for its work. Riding high on legal success, it is sometimes difficult to contemplate that a compliance failure or a lack of attention to risk management could bring that enviable reputation tumbling down.

The last 10 years have seen a massive increase in regulation of the Bar,[1] yet of all the professional services, the Bar is probably one of the least heavily regulated. Observance of the Bar Code of Conduct, now included in the Bar Standards Board (BSB) Handbook,[2] is engrained in the psyche of all barristers, although awareness of the detail is generally a bit vague. The BSB regulatory regime tries to be proportionate to the risks it needs to regulate and has implemented a 'light touch' approach with an emphasis on guidance, self-assessment and support through supervision. Regulation is not high on the list of concerns of most practitioners, but there has been an important change in recent years which should be noted. The BSB rules[3] now make all barristers in a set "responsible for the competent and efficient administration" of that chambers and for "having appropriate risk management procedures in place and being complied with". With professional non-clerking staff being employed in many sets, legal and regulatory requirements are more likely to be implemented effectively and kept under review. Nonetheless, barristers cannot escape responsibility for ensuring, directly or indirectly, that their organisation is well run and meets its obligations. The responsibility for ensuring that a chambers is compliant is now a collective one.

---

1   There are three primary regulators relevant to barristers: the Bar Council which represents the interests of the Bar on all matters relating to the profession and remains the 'Approved Regulator' in the Legal Services Act 2007, but has delegated its regulatory functions to the BSB, the independent regulator for the Bar with supervision and enforcement responsibility; and the Legal Services Board, which has an overarching responsibility for regulation of the legal profession as a whole and to whom the BSB, Bar Council, Solicitors Regulation Authority and others are accountable.
2   www.barstandardsboard.org.uk/regulatory-requirements.
3   www.barstandardsboard.org.uk/regulatory-requirements rC89–rC90, pages 66–67.

In addition to regulatory responsibilities, chambers, like other business organisations, must comply with legal requirements from employment law (including immigration issues), to legislation under the Companies Act (particularly as it impacts on service companies and alternative business structures), to health and safety. Of major importance to lawyers is information governance and data protection. At the time of writing, the General Data Protection Regulation (GDPR) is soon to be enforced; and the ePrivacy Regulation is also expected to apply from late May 2018. The former in particular brings a new legal framework that will expand and tighten up rules on the processing of personal data to provide regulatory consistency at European level. It is expected to impose significant penalties should there be a breach of data security.

This chapter does not aim to cover every regulatory requirement for a chambers; it will focus on some of the more recent changes, and those that need special mention. It will look at some of the threats to reputation and how to minimise risks and go about damage limitation. It will consider how to approach compliance and risk management and the benefits of being proactive.

2. Threats to reputation: non-compliance

For a barrister there are some obvious and completely avoidable pitfalls, and avoiding them starts with observing BSB Handbook rules on all relevant aspects of practice. The BSB requires that all practitioners, including second and third six pupils, have a current practising (or provisional practising) certificate and professional insurance in place, while the Information Commissioner's Office (ICO) expects practitioners to be registered with it as data controllers when processing personal data (unless an exemption applies) – a requirement under the Data Protection Act 1998 (soon to be replaced by a new act). The ICO has issued guidance, which is available on its website.[4] The scope and nature of the ICO notification process will change under the GDPR. Some chambers will organise all of this so that all renewals are done together, others may manage some or none of these. In whatever way these requirements are managed, it is always the barrister's responsibility to ensure that these essential elements to practice are up to date. As all barristers know, they each have an obligation to run their practices competently and to ensure that their conduct with regard to their clients, conduct in court and fee management complies with professional standards. Moreover, where they see those standards not being met, and that failure could amount to serious misconduct, barristers have a duty[5] to report other barristers to the BSB. They also need to note that it is a serious misconduct matter if a barrister fails to report serious misconduct promptly to the BSB.

Continuing professional development (CPD) has gone through various incarnations in recent years and the emphasis is currently on outcomes with a less prescriptive approach as to how these are achieved. Failure to complete CPD can result in corrective action or a referral to the Bar Standards Board's Professional Conduct Department for enforcement action. All practising barristers who have completed the

---

4   https://ico.org.uk/media/for-organisations/documents/1578/registration-of-barristers-chambers.pdf.
5   BSB Handbook C66 to C69 and Guidance C95 to C101.

first three years of practice are required to undertake the Established Practitioners Programme (EPP), which no longer specifies a minimum number of hours required and allows for non-BSB accredited training. Each barrister must prepare and implement their own CPD plan by 31 December each year and make a declaration that they have done this at the time they renew their practising certificate. The fact that barristers do not have to automatically submit their CPD plan may lead some to let the process slide. A spot check by the BSB for plans going back up to three years could induce embarrassment, not to say panic, if the documentation and activity are not in place. Heads of chambers could also be implicated in any CPD breach as the BSB has issued guidance[6] suggesting that the organisation has a responsibility to oversee barrister CPD activities. Some chambers ask an administrator or clerk to record training and chase tenants for CPD records – a thankless task that wastes a good deal of staff time – in order to meet this responsibility. There is a different CPD programme for those with under three years' practice (the New Practitioners' Programme (NPP)), but much of the above still pertains.

There is little excuse for any barrister not to be familiar with, and observant of, good equality and diversity (E&D) practice and to operate wholly within the law on matters such as recruitment, employment and maternity rights as applied to staff, pupils and barristers. The Bar Council has dedicated years to trying to raise awareness among barristers and their staff on these issues and E&D training is held regularly. Not only does it make good business sense to encourage and support a diverse profession through fair recruitment procedures and an enlightened approach, but for middle and senior juniors there is the added value of being comfortable with the language and issues of E&D in preparation for QC applications and interviews. While the Bar Council has produced its comprehensive *Fair Recruitment Guide* to assist barristers and chambers, the BSB Handbook requires compliance with the Equality Rules[7] covering issues of monitoring, diversity data and reporting, recruitment, fair access to work, policy development and action plans.

Under the Equality Rules, chambers must appoint at least one equality and diversity officer (EDO). In order for this appointment to be meaningful this should be someone with a demonstrable commitment to promoting good practice and with sufficient authority to be heard in chambers and bring about change where required. The EDO is there to monitor chambers' performance of its compliance duties, raise awareness of diversity issues, recommend action and ensure that chambers has in place an anti-harassment policy, a parental leave policy, a flexible working policy (applicable to members of chambers, managers or employees so that they can manage their family responsibilities or disability without giving up work), and a reasonable adjustments policy. As part of the role, the EDO may have access to an analysis of income, billings and aged debt figures, recruitment statistics and allocation of work reports. For this reason the appointment is one of trust and a senior practitioner is more likely to be able to command the respect that the role requires if it is to be effective. Delegating a junior practitioner to this responsibility, without providing

---

6   www.barstandardsboard.org.uk/media/1800831/head_of_chambers_cpd_guidance.pdf.
7   www.barstandardsboard.org.uk/regulatory-requirements rC110.

proper support and reporting processes, could suggest that the duty is not being taken seriously and that there is a lack of concern about the need to make progress.

Fair recruitment training is now a standard requirement for all barristers who may be involved in selection processes. This is not just about interviews, which must be conducted in line with good practice; it also includes shortlisting procedures. Fair recruitment training can be completed by a barrister self-certifying that s/he has read and understood the BSB's *Equality Guide*; however, this is a minimum requirement and without dedicated time and training may be of limited value. Records must be kept (of how and when training took place) by the individual or by the organisation, and barristers must have undertaken training within the five years preceding the selection/recruitment process they are involved in. Some sets record details of when barristers undertake this training in order to ensure that they are complying with regulatory requirements and the BSB can request evidence that the chambers is compliant with this duty.

In an effort to ensure that, as far as possible, unnamed casework coming into chambers is fairly allocated between suitable barristers, there is now a regulatory duty to monitor how this is done. The data on how unassigned work is allocated to members should be made available to the chambers' EDO who should analyse and report on it internally. Both the recording and the monitoring of how unallocated work is distributed can be an onerous task. Although there is software functionality available through the fees and diary systems, the recording process is time consuming, particularly if sets receive a large volume of unallocated work or enquiries. The data cannot account for all of the variables that present in different situations and it is the case that the data is only monitoring one aspect of practice development. Nonetheless, it is a requirement to monitor this work and it is an important first step in trying to eliminate unconscious or conscious bias and promote good practice. Chambers might also review fee income, billings and aged debt by call band for practitioners with anonymised protected characteristics, as well as career progression, particularly into silk but also into directory listings.

Currently, diversity data on tenants must be reviewed and updated every three years. Chambers must also have in place a diversity data officer (DDO) who will ensure that there is a policy on how diversity data will be collected and used. Although individual barristers are not obligated to provide data, and the DDO must make it clear that providing data is voluntary, the chambers is required to invite all members to complete a model questionnaire covering protected characteristics, educational background, social mobility and caring responsibilities, and publish the results on its website (or make them available on request if the set does not have a website). Because there is no obligation to complete the survey, many barristers do not do it. This can result in some very misleading statistics about the composition of chambers, some of which are then reproduced as fact in the legal press. It is outcomes like these that have led the Legal Services Board (LSB) to move from a prescriptive approach to regulatory activity to one based on outcomes.[8] The BSB will still have to

---

8   www.legalservicesboard.org.uk/what_we_do/consultations/closed/pdf/20170215/2017_Encouraging_A_Diverse_Workforce.pdf.

collect diversity data for the profession to inform regulatory and policy decisions and will be encouraged to take their responsibilities 'beyond data collection'. The model questionnaire has been removed from LSB guidance to regulators. However, at the time of writing, the BSB requirement on chambers to provide statistics on the composition of chambers for public information using this questionnaire has not been amended.

All sets must have a written action plan on how to promote E&D within their chambers. The action plan is important because it requires some analysis of where the chambers is in terms of its awareness, culture and diversity, and what needs to be done to address any gaps. There is a personal obligation on all barristers to take 'reasonable steps' to ensure that the Equality Rules are being observed in chambers. The action plan, if agreed and monitored by chambers, is one way of checking that the organisation is both complying and moving forward.

Every chambers must have a process in place for handling complaints[9] and for informing lay clients of their right to make a complaint and how to go about it.[10] Chambers are expected to provide these details direct to the lay client and not to rely on the solicitor to relay the information. This continues to be problematic for the simple reason that barristers often do not have contact details for the lay client. Nonetheless the outcome required is that lay clients must be able to find out how to make a complaint with ease and there would be a case to answer if a client approached the Bar Council or BSB because they could not work out who to complain to. An acceptable mix should be a combination of informing the lay client directly where that is possible, requesting solicitors to pass on complaints details in their contracts and engagement letters, leaflets or other client care publicity in the chambers, and details on the website. The complaints policy or procedure should be in plain English and should be accessible to all, including vulnerable people and those with special needs. This means, at minimum, that complaints can be received by email, letter or telephone. The complaints procedure should identify who to contact, how the complaint will be dealt with and by whom, how long it will take, and what happens next; this should include possible options if the complaint is upheld and signposting to the Legal Ombudsman if it is not. The policy should also inform clients that alternative dispute resolution (ADR) is available to them[11] if their complaint is not resolved through the chambers' complaints process and identify an appropriate ADR approved body,[12] although chambers are not, in fact, required to forward complaints to the body. If a client is referred to the Legal Ombudsman, they

---

9   www.barstandardsboard.org.uk/code-guidance/first-tier-complaints-handling/.
10   Section 112 of the Legal Services Act, Chapter 3.2 of the Legal Ombudsman Scheme Rules; BSB rules on notifying the lay client of how to make a complaint.
11   Directive 2013/11/EU on alternative dispute resolution for consumer disputes and amending Regulation (EC) No 2006/2004 and Directive 2009/22/EC http://eur-lex.europa.eu/legal-content/EN/TXT/?uri=celex:32013L0011.
     The Alternative Dispute Resolution for Consumer Disputes (Competent Authorities and Information) Regulations 2015 No 542 www.legislation.gov.uk/uksi/2015/542 and The Alternative Dispute Resolution for Consumer Disputes (Amendment) Regulations 2015 No 1392 www.legislation.gov.uk/uksi/2015/1392.
12   www.barstandardsboard.org.uk/media/1704682/alternative_dispute_resolution_for_consumer_disputes__amendment__regulations_2015_guidance.pdf.

should be told that the service is free and independent, what the timescales are for bringing a complaint and how to contact the Ombudsman. It is worth noting that even if there is nothing in a complaint, the way in which a matter is handled can lead to action being taken by the Ombudsman.

The BSB is currently [October 2017] reviewing the rules on handling complaints as part of the consultation on transparency standards.[13] In October 2017, the BSB wrote in its response to the Competition and Market Authority's Recommendations:

> In relation to complaints process and access to the LeO, there are some existing requirements in place in the Handbook to which barristers need to adhere. After barristers have been instructed, Rule C99.1 of the BSB Handbook requires them to inform clients in writing of their right to make a complaint, including any right to complain to the LeO. Rule C103 also states that chambers' websites must display information about the chambers' complaints procedure. These rules may need to be amended to ensure that the client has access to all the necessary information in relation to complaints before instructing a barrister (including the right to complain to the LeO).[14]

In other words, it is likely to become a requirement that all information on how to make a complaint that chambers currently provide to clients after barristers have been instructed, including the right to complain to the Legal Ombudsman, will need to be publicly available at all times.

The BSB, and increasingly clients, expect chambers to be able to evidence that they have a proactive, proportionate approach to managing risk and compliance. The BSB gathers that evidence through a supervision process to ensure that a chambers is managing its risk and responsibilities in five core areas: governance and administration; provision of services to clients; equality and diversity; pupillage; and financial management. The BSB leaves open the option to focus on one or more aspects of compliance in future supervision depending on regulatory developments and perceived need. In 2015, when the first supervision exercise was conducted, it was anticipated that this would be carried out every three years.

The risk assessment process starts with a detailed questionnaire, an Impact Audit Survey, which, even with all relevant policies in place, requires considerable time to complete. This is not a task that can be delegated to a junior member of staff and responses must correspond to the operation of chambers in practice. Supervision Returns to the BSB may be followed by supervision visits designed to gather more information about how a chambers operates and these visits can be informed by seeking information from other sources, including the Legal Ombudsman and the BSB's Professional Conduct Department.

Once the Impact Audit Survey has been completed, a chambers will be grouped into one of three categories according to impact: Low, Medium or High Impact. The BSB makes clear that "there is very little that a chambers can do to reduce their impact score as it will be inherent to the activities and profile of chambers". Those

13   www.barstandardsboard.org.uk/media/1852551/october_2017_-_policy_consultation_on_transparency_ standards.pdf. Note that the BSB is also looking at transparency in respect of fees and services.
14   www.barstandardsboard.org.uk/media/1852551/october_2017_-_policy_consultation_on_ transparency_standards.pdf p26.

categorised as High and Medium Impact attract most attention from the BSB, which is keen to minimise risk across the profession. A large set, perhaps with annexes, could be more difficult to manage; the structure and business model of the chambers could impact on how it operates internally and externally; a chambers that has set up an entity, runs an escrow account or undertakes work within the scope of the Money Laundering Regulations has specific legal and regulatory obligations; sets that take pupils run a higher regulatory risk than those that do not; the number of cases conducted by a set and the nature of that work, and in particular how much public access work is undertaken, are also variables which contribute to the overall assessment of regulatory impact.

The BSB then factors in how well a chambers manages risk in the context of their 'impact' score. So, a chambers that has a large vulnerable client base and conducts significant amounts of public access work will be assessed as High Impact. However, if that chambers has an excellent approach to client care, with clear contractual terms, accessible information and guidance, well-trained staff, and a complaints process which is demonstrably thorough and fair, then the BSB is likely to assess that aspect of the chambers' business as Low Risk. This means that the chambers has done everything it reasonably can to alleviate the risk of things going wrong with this aspect of their operation and if something does go wrong, then it is anticipated that it will deal with it effectively. Similarly, if a chambers undertakes work within the scope of the Money Laundering Regulations, a High Impact activity, the BSB will take into account whether an officer with suitable experience and authority has been appointed and properly trained, anti-money laundering and fraud prevention business checks are carried out, and policies and processes for managing and monitoring accounts and the transfer of monies are in place, before reaching a risk score. A chambers can be High Impact and Low Risk.

All sets assessed as Low Risk are unlikely to be followed up by the BSB until the next assessment, unless the Supervision Team becomes aware of any evidence that suggests further action is required. This allows the BSB to target its resources at those most likely to be, or become, non-compliant. Medium or High Risk sets should expect to be contacted by the BSB Supervision Team, which will identify the weaknesses to be addressed and by when. The BSB currently provides proactive supervision in the form of direction and guidance with the aim of preventing non-compliance problems before they happen. The BSB also takes into account matters such as disciplinary history and good practice measures. A referral to the Professional Conduct Department (and subsequent enforcement action) is reserved for the most serious cases – for example, if non-compliance is not dealt with within a reasonable or specified timeframe, there is a history of non-cooperation and non-compliance, or there is considered to be a major non-compliance issue.

An area of legal compliance that could leave a chambers exposed is in relation to immigration status and right to work checks. Rule changes have potential implications for the recruitment of tenants, pupils and short-term placements who are not UK or European nationals. The Bar Council is licensed by UK Visas and Immigration (UKVI) as a Government Approved Sponsor under Tier 5 of the points-based system for work-related immigration (Government Approved Exchange). It also acts as a Sponsor for Tier 2 (General) visa purposes. Chambers wanting to recruit non-EEA workers to fill vacancies under a Tier 2 General visa have to make declarations of compliance to the Bar Council that the chambers has met the requirements of the Home Office's Resident Labour Market Test (RLMT) and must supply documentation from the relevant recruitment round to back that up. There are several points worth noting about this process. Home Office rules are designed for employers, and the guidance repeatedly refers to employers; this could lead a chambers to conclude that the rules are not applicable to it but this would be wrong; these rules are definitely applicable to the recruitment of tenants and pupils.

To be in a position to offer a migrant from outside the EEA a funded pupillage, a chambers would have to have first conducted a prescribed, open recruitment process that complies with the UKVI's requirements of the RLMT (unless a limited range of exemptions apply). The prescribed process usually means that chambers would be required to advertise vacancies in at least two specified media for a minimum period of 28 calendar days as stated in the relevant guidance.[15] They need to see if the job can be filled by a UK or EEA national before the job can be offered to someone from outside the EEA. It is important to note that where both a settled person and a migrant have applied for the vacancy, a Tier 2 sponsor cannot hire the migrant solely due to the fact that s/he is more experienced ("If you find that you have more than one candidate with all the necessary skills and experience you advertised for, where one is a settled worker and the other a migrant, you must appoint the settled worker even if the migrant is more skilled or experienced" – page 115 of the UKVI guidance for sponsors on Tiers 2 & 5, version 11/16). The migrant must be the only qualified candidate for the role in order to proceed with sponsorship. If a chambers reaches the point where it wants to recruit a non-EEA pupil or tenant and it has not observed the UKVI rules[16] up until that point, it may be too late to gather the evidence required to make a successful application. Chambers must also ensure that the pupil or tenant has, or is applying for, the correct visa status. Chambers must monitor their status in compliance with the rules because there is a duty to inform the Bar Council and the UKVI if relevant circumstances change. There are costs involved in making the application for both the individual and a chambers and, importantly, some elements of those costs (Immigration Skills Charge) cannot be transferred to the pupil or tenant.

According to a 2017 study conducted by the Ponemon Institute[17] which assessed the reputational impact of data breaches for US companies, 81% of respondents said that a breach would affect their organisation's economic value, while the average value of a brand as a direct result of a breach diminished by 21%. It took an average of nearly a year to restore a company's reputation. Data protection and privacy present significant challenges for barristers and chambers, particularly with the enforcement of the GDPR from 25 May 2018. Data security and privacy breaches happen in all business areas, but in a profession where much data is highly sensitive the unauthorised leak, loss of or damage to personal data could destroy or seriously

---

15   www.gov.uk/government/collections/sponsorship-information-for-employers-and-educators.
16   www.gov.uk/government/uploads/system/uploads/attachment_data/file/616206/Tier_25_guidance_05-2017.pdf.
17   www.ponemon.org/library/2017-cost-of-data-breach-study-united-states.

damage a reputation based on trust. The context is also one where huge amounts of personal data are still in hard copy being trolleyed around the streets of major cities and the difficulty for chambers in ensuring that self-employed barristers fully comply with data protection protocols. It will take only one barrister to have a major data security breach for his chambers to suffer the consequences. Tenders for panel work are likely to require disclosure of reportable incidents. A chambers could become a focus for in-depth attention from the BSB Supervision Team and the ICO. There may be formal complaints and there could be significant fines, which would not be covered by insurance because you cannot be compensated for breaking the law. However, the biggest problem would be reputational damage. The Government Legal Service, in-house counsel, insurers, solicitors – no supplier of work could easily justify instructing an individual, and perhaps the chambers, known to have seriously compromised client privacy.

It is anticipated that under the GDPR, certain types of data breach will be reportable to the ICO as the lead supervisory authority in the United Kingdom and, in some circumstances (where a breach is likely to result in a high risk to the rights and freedoms of individuals), to the data subjects themselves, who are most likely to be chambers' solicitors or lay clients. This will not just be about self-reporting by barristers or chambers as data controllers; persons or entities, including chambers, that process data on behalf of data controllers will be identified as data processors and data processors will have a duty to report non-compliance in line with the regulation. Data breaches must be reported by a data controller to the ICO without undue delay, and not later than 72 hours after becoming aware of the breach, and those appointed as data processor(s) will be directly liable under the regulation if they fail to meet the standards of the regulation. Chambers will also need to decide whether it needs to appoint a data protection officer; at the time of writing it is suggested that it would be unusual for a set to be required to appoint one.[18] Whether or not it does, chambers will need to be clear about who carries out data controller, data processor or, if needed, data protection officer responsibilities. Whoever performs these roles must be in a position to fulfil the legal obligations, including avoiding conflicts of interest, even though there may be severe consequences for an individual or for the chambers. The Bar Council has issued guidance to the Bar[19] in October 2017, and the ICO also has a range of guidance on its website.

Potential breaches may be caused by not disposing of confidential documents securely, by leaving them where unauthorised persons can view them, or by losing data perhaps because case papers have been sent to the wrong place or an unencrypted laptop without appropriate authentication was left on a train. Leaving papers on an unattended desk or on a photocopier, which many barristers do, even presents a potential risk. Additionally, all data, not just current data, must be properly held. Information held on any person must be accurate and wholly relevant to their relationship with chambers and the circumstances of their connection. This

---

18   http://live.barcouncil.netxtra.net/practice-ethics/professional-practice-and-ethics/it-issues/gdpr-guide-for-barristers-and-chambers/.

19   *Ibid.*

means that staff and barristers will have to ensure that they do not have historical data that should have been deleted or destroyed.

This chapter is about the risks faced by the Bar, but not all members of the Bar practise from a chambers and some chambers have set up, or have made provision for individuals to set up, entities and alternative business structures (see the following paragraph below). Individual self-employed barristers may operate as sole practitioners if they have three or more years' practice following pupillage; before then they must work with a 'qualified person' or have the requirement waived by the BSB. They must inform the Bar Council of their new practice contact details and confirm that they have appropriate professional insurance cover for all legal services they intend to undertake. If they anticipate sharing office space and facilities they should check the BSB "Associations with Others" Rules.[20] All aspects of practice must be efficiently managed, they must comply with BSB duties, and all policies must be in place relevant to their operation. Individual practitioners are subject to BSB supervision arrangements, although not all may be contacted. They are likely to be assessed as Low Impact because the risk is confined to a fairly small client base and any reputational damage is to the sole practitioner. This does not mean that sole practitioners will not be assessed as High Risk.

Supervision also applies to BSB authorised bodies ('entities'), which are owned and managed by practising barristers (and other lawyers), and BSB licensed bodies, Alternative Business Structures (ABSs), which are owned and managed jointly by lawyers and non-lawyers. ABSs and entities must manage their own risks well and comply with their regulatory obligations.[21] This includes ensuring a number of policies are in place, including: client care; fraud/bribery; barrister training and CPD; whistleblowing; money laundering and terrorist financing; and a finance policy.

If a chambers is considering setting up its own BSB regulated entity, perhaps to brand a niche service or for registering with international bodies, it will need to consider a number of issues, including whether the creation of an entity will cause conflict issues for members of chambers, whether the entity will be profit-making and, if so, how those profits will be distributed, and whether the entity will be held in trust for all members. It is worth checking the cost of cover with professional insurance companies at an early stage to get an idea of premiums. BSB regulated entities will be required to appoint a head of legal practice (HOLP) and head of finance and administration (HOFA), but they will not be permitted to manage clients' money, which significantly reduces the risk exposure for entities. An escrow account will be required and the Bar Council has an existing scheme which offers a streamlined service. Chambers will need to consider the business model for its entity and matters such as whether the entity seeks to conduct litigation or whether it will need to register with Companies House and provide audited accounts.

More difficult to manage is the situation where a member or a group of members in chambers want to set up an entity independently. The chambers will want to ensure that work being conducted through the new entity is not work that would

---

20   BSB Handbook, Rules C79–C85.
21   BSB Handbook rS101 and rS102.

have been otherwise processed through chambers and on which a levy would have been charged. Alternatively, the new entity might be providing services which compete with those offered by chambers. Some members may want to set up companies through which to manage their finances for tax reasons; this could be particularly relevant to any barristers based in Europe and concerned about the possibility of being taxed twice after Brexit. What constitutional arrangements could be set up to accommodate new entities? How would chambers respond to finding out that a member was already channelling casework through an entity? What risks could a chambers face if an entity managed by some members was found to be in breach of regulatory or legal requirements?

Barristers who want to undertake public access or licensed access work must ensure that they have the necessary skills, experience and training before accepting any instructions on that basis. Legal aid work cannot be conducted through public access but a client entitled to legal aid could, in exceptional circumstances, instruct a barrister under the public access scheme if it was clearly in their interest to do so. Self-employed barristers are allowed to apply for an extension to their practising certificate in order to be able to conduct litigation.

Websites and social media present numerous risks for chambers. The BSB requires that marketing rules are not breached by an individual or a chambers by stating that they are the pre-eminent set at the Bar or in their field of work on their website or other media. The BSB Handbook requires complaints information and diversity data to be published on websites, as well as details of the basis on which legal services are being offered. This:

> may be achieved by including a reference or link to the relevant terms in your written communication of acceptance. You may, for example, refer the client or professional client (as the case may be) to the terms of service set out on your website or to standard terms of service set out on the Bar Council's website.[22]

Data protection law requires that organisations inform people how their personal data is processed and chambers' websites should contain relevant information, such as: whether cookies are in operation, the scope of personal data collected, and, if so, how it is used and/or shared, and retained; the nature of third-party services being utilised; and what other information is collected. In addition, chambers are obliged to publish details of their operation under the Provision of Services Regulations 2009.[23]

Social media raises numerous risk issues and it is advisable to organise briefings and put in place a policy for staff and barristers about acceptable use. Does chambers allow, or even encourage, staff to tweet and post messages on behalf of the organisation? Are disclaimers required? What view will heads and managers take of social media comments detrimental to chambers, whether intentional or accidental? The BSB points out a less obvious risk: "by advertising the fact that you are in a particular location at a particular time (perhaps via a "geotagged" status update), you may risk inadvertently revealing that you acted for a particular client."[24]

---

22   BSB Handbook C75.
23   www.barcouncil.org.uk/media/437394/the_provision_of_services_regulations_2009.pdf.
24   www.barstandardsboard.org.uk/media/1821624/bsb_social_media_guidance_pdf.

3. Business continuity

Business continuity involves anticipating interruptions to service and preparing to respond effectively to any incident that impacts on the provision of chambers' services. Incidents could be caused by resource issues such as telephony or IT breakdowns, weather events such as snow or flooding, or disasters which can disrupt business operation for a few hours or up to several months. Disasters, by their very nature, are random events and therefore difficult to anticipate. It is therefore more useful to consider how you would respond to types and levels of impact rather than speculate about the types of incident that may give rise to a disaster scenario. Chambers might want to consider plans for minor disruption of up to 24 hours; medium disruption extending beyond 24 hours (or no damage but no access to chambers); serious damage which includes when one or more systems on which chambers depends is out of action; up to catastrophic damage which may destroy systems, facilities or data, cause injury or death, and make it extremely difficult for the organisation to recover.

In any emergency the priorities for senior management are likely to be to ensure the health and safety of all users of chambers, ensure the security of chambers' premises and data where necessary and possible, provide information to those who may be affected by the incident, and restore services as quickly and efficiently as possible. To achieve this, some element of planning must already be in place because time is of the essence in a crisis and it cannot be assumed that everyone will know what to do or who will be in charge. An office manual which details all aspects of how chambers' facilities and operations are maintained can be combined with plans that document approaches and responsibilities in different situations. Ensuring that those documents are available in hard copy and also kept at home by key people in chambers can help to deal with situations such as: how to communicate quickly to everyone in chambers that there is a problem even if the IT system or telephone system is out of action; who keeps emergency contact details of users, suppliers and emergency support, and where; how to communicate to clients when the website and telephony systems may not be functioning; which staff can work at home and which staff and barristers are most important to resolving the crisis; at what point to consider moving business activities to another venue (an annex, rented offices, another chambers); and what financial and insurance arrangements are in place to aid recovery. Keeping the plan focused but flexible, and allowing for judgement and common sense to prevail, are advisable.

4. Other risks

Consider: how would your head(s) or chambers management committee deal with a member bringing a complaint of discrimination? Or a case of bullying? How would they react if an employee breached confidentiality on social media or a senior member committed a serious data security breach? How would it cope in the face of a professional or financial scandal? What if a group of the highest earners in chambers left to go elsewhere? By anticipating the kinds of risk that all organisations potentially face, chambers can work backwards and ask questions such as: what disciplinary provisions are in the Constitution, including suspension and expulsion?

Does the Constitution provide for the imposition of additional levies? Does the Constitution deal with the wind-up of chambers? Are grievance and complaints procedures fit for purpose? In what circumstances might a chambers need a PR company? Is there provision in the budget for independent professional services for employment and other legal advice, legal action and PR crisis communications? Are these just for chambers or are they available to individual practitioners? Does the insurance policy cover criminal activity, cybercrime or management liability? Does chambers have evidence of good practice through certification or quality standards? Where is chambers' data stored and how well is it protected? Are chambers' accounts audited and, if not, what financial monitoring and validation is in place? How has the social media policy been communicated through chambers and how effective has training on phishing risks been?

Who has responsibility for making sure that these things are in place? At a practical level the tasks of development of policy and good practice, and the assessment of risk, lie with senior staff. However, all barristers in the chambers can be held ultimately responsible for regulatory breaches and all barristers are at risk from crises. It is therefore important that chambers is satisfied that high standards are being met, and that monitoring and reporting duties are properly delegated to individual, and groups of, barristers, including evaluating the consequences of not assessing risk. Those individuals must not only have the authority to expose any risks – otherwise they cannot be held accountable – but they must also feel that the culture in chambers is such that the heads or management committee will value the opportunity to address those risks. In turn the decision-makers need to understand what risks they are prepared to take: there may be some risks which are worth running because addressing them is not affordable or not a high priority for chambers.

Training on compliance issues is fundamental to managing risk. If staff and barristers understand, and do, what is required of them to comply with regulatory obligations, then chambers minimises risk. Where there is a regulation that affects the way a chambers operates then employees should have some knowledge and training on it. Management must allocate time and money to ensure that regulatory objectives are being met and if it does not happen the chambers management committee or head(s) of chambers need to be reminded that they are ultimately responsible for ensuring compliance, and this includes training.

For some crises, such as a major phishing incident or an allegation of sexual harassment, an immediate response that is robust and confident will suggest an organisation taking control. Where a regulatory breach has occurred, swift reporting backed up by evidence of action being taken will provide reassurance that the matter is being dealt with responsibly. Some crises – or apparent crises – may be handled more effectively with no early response or disclosure, but the risk of an incident becoming public or requiring a response should be prepared for. Whatever the immediate response it is important to ensure that communications with all relevant stakeholders are open and clear; lack of information, or misinformation, at a time of crisis can result in panic, confusion and/or a loss of morale.

5. Integrated approach

Properly managing regulatory and other risks is time consuming and comes at a cost, but should be considered an integral part of the management function. Anyone who has managed a complaints process for chambers or who has had to undertake a data subject access request will know that these tasks can absorb a significant amount of management time. However, they will also know that much more time is taken up if there is no clear process to follow and the task is performed *ad hoc* or without adequate resources. In the past chambers have not always invested enough in compliance, but legal and regulatory requirements in recent years have made this an imperative. The long-term cost of not putting sufficient resources into managing risk (emerging risks as well as those we currently deal with) could be substantial.

The assessment of risk is a chambers-wide issue and ideally involves an integrated approach across all levels of the organisation, led by the head or management committee, and the senior managers. It is all too easy to compartmentalise risk and put nominal policies in place only for some key aspects of chambers business; this may ensure, for instance, that the organisation complies with regulatory requirements on paper but it is not a proper assessment of the risk that a chambers may be running. Risk management is part of good governance, which is about effective, ethical leadership and management that protects the financial, reputational and psychological wellbeing of chambers. Good governance ensures that the strategy, business plans and structures suit chambers' needs. It is assisted by transparent decision-making, oversight of implementation and good communications. Good governance builds a culture in which the values of the organisation are lived, as part of normal day-to-day working, where good practice is the norm, and where the values of the organisation underpin and strengthen the commitment to chambers, and make people in the organisation feel positive. With a culture that reinforces the collective sense of direction it is easier to engage chambers people on risks and how to mitigate them.

6. Evaluation of risk

When chambers consider risk they should be looking at the potential loss or damage that would be caused by something going wrong, and how effectively they can deal with it and remain competitive. Although risk management teaches us to expect the unexpected, except for interruptions to service many of the common risks faced by a chambers can be anticipated. Those risks that arise from legislation, regulation, breaches of good practice and quality standards involve non-compliance actions and most can be prevented or mitigated with more training, enforcement, investment or staffing. Those risks that emerge from a lack of consensus in chambers or a shift in the market are more nebulous but they are familiar to the profession and chambers do have options about how they choose to deal with them. There are also the risks that organisations take when they do something innovative such as opening an annex, setting up a new entity or investing in an international initiative; chambers are not always good at properly analysing the direct and indirect costs of such ventures, the anticipated return on the investment and the long-term impact on the whole organisation.

The process of evaluating risk for a chambers is, in most cases, fairly straightforward. It can be achieved by multiplying the consequence of a risk with the likelihood of it happening and giving that risk a value which determines how significant it is and how much effort should go into dealing with it. The consequences of something going wrong for chambers can be measured in terms of financial damage and reputational damage and so these are separately assessed and added together. Using a basic table and the following formula a chambers can begin to evaluate the risks it faces:

Objectives	Possible Risks	Financial Impact	Reputational Impact	Likelihood	Risk Level	Priority	Action required, when and by whom
HR policies comply with HR legislation and best practice. Chambers is recognised as a responsible and progressive employer.	Inconsistent or illegal approach to HR. Lowering of staff morale. Grievances from staff or risk of legal action against chambers and barristers. Damage to reputation. Loss of good staff and cost of replacement.	2	2.5	1.5	6.75	House keeping	Ongoing review of policies by Management Committee; Staffing Committee report on automated HR software and the London Living Wage to be considered in Jan 2018.

Allocate 1 (low), 2 (medium) or 3 (high) under financial impact, damage to reputation and likelihood of happening
Calculate Risk = financial impact + impact on reputation × likelihood of happening
Risk Level: 3-5: Low Risk; 6-8: Housekeeping (keep under review); 9-11 Contingency (needs addressing); 12+: Significant (immediate action required)

In this scenario the heading could be Staffing or Human Resources, or perhaps Governance, and this might be one of several objectives in this category. This is a set that wants to be seen as a progressive employer; therefore the reputational damage could be greater than in a set whose priorities are elsewhere. In this scenario the risk level is fairly low and the action required is limited. However, in other areas of chambers' operation the risk level could be much higher. Take, for example, the GDPR:

Objectives	Possible Risks	Financial Impact	Reputational Impact	Likelihood	Risk Level	Priority	Action required, when and by whom
Policy and practice to comply with GDPR legislation and best practice.	Delay in addressing new legislation means insufficient time to plan properly causing pressure on time and resources. Possibility of not being prepared in time and running risk of an error which puts spotlight on chambers. Cannot demonstrate good preparation and practice in the event of a data security breach.	3	3	2.5	15	Significant	A draft project management plan to be put in place immediately by X and presented to the Management Committee by X. Distribute guidance to all members.
Gap analysis and data inventory is drawn up so that we understand what data we hold individually, and as an organisation, and can take steps to protect it.	Insufficient involvement of all stakeholders leads to an ineffective data audit process. Some data continues to be collected and utilised outside of the new framework. Additional work created in short term. Potential reputational damage and financial penalty if data is not captured in audit process.	3	3	2.5	15	Significant	See project management plan. X to set up meetings with all key staff; X to set up meetings with all barristers and pupils by dd/mm/yy. Draft gap analysis and data inventory to be in place by dd/mm/yy.

continued on next page

Objectives	Possible Risks	Financial Impact	Reputational Impact	Likelihood	Risk Level	Priority	Action required, when and by whom
(If considered necessary) The appointment of a DPO who will report directly to the Management Committee.	Appointment does not have sufficient knowledge of the GDPR and the role, or the resources necessary, or does not have the will/ authority to act independently if necessary. A DPO is compromised or overruled.	2	3	2	10	Contingency	Management Committee to consider all potential candidates for this role asap and organise training.
Ownership of, and accountability for, data are well understood throughout chambers.	Staff and members have vague idea of what they must do or a few have not engaged and are a risk to chambers. Mistakes happen and must be reported. Cannot evidence good practice. Large fines are imposed. Barristers lose credibility, staff lose jobs. Chambers' reputation damaged.	3	3	2			

continued on next page

Objectives	Possible Risks	Financial Impact	Reputational Impact	Likelihood	Risk Level	Priority	Action required, when and by whom
Chambers has procedures to follow in the event of a personal data breach, which take account of the new notification requirements.	Panic about how to manage a data breach and who should be taking a lead. Time is wasted. The response is uncoordinated and considered inadequate by the ICO. Data subjects express concern and dissatisfaction. Exposure by press and media is poorly handled. Chambers' reputation is damaged. ICO more likely to impose large fines.						

Allocate 1 (low), 2 (medium) or 3 (high) under financial impact, damage to reputation and likelihood of happening

Calculate Risk = financial impact + impact on reputation × likelihood of happening

Risk Level: 3-5: Low Risk; 6-8: Housekeeping (keep under review); 9-11 Contingency (needs addressing); 12+: Significant (immediate action required)

In this instance there are some significant risks which need urgent action and a project management plan should be put in place to manage each stage of the compliance process, paying attention to each of the potential risks identified. One of the dangers is to produce an assessment like this, identify an individual or committee who should deal with it, and assume that this is now dealt with. Particularly where a risk is high, it is important to understand the roles and responsibilities of everyone affected and make sure that appropriate plans are put in place.

The big picture must include strategic direction and governance. There are major risks to the cohesion of chambers if members do not have confidence in the leadership of chambers, trust that the organisation is being properly managed, and support what the set is trying to achieve. All organisations have their good times and bad times; in a chambers with numerous barristers many of the bad times are the result of differences of approach, disagreement about priorities, worries about how chambers is working and the future of chambers. Taking a detailed look at all aspects of how chambers is operating provides an opportunity to acknowledge what is working and see where the problems and challenges are. The emphasis will vary between sets but a holistic approach might also cover: tenancy recruitment; service standards and client care; financial planning and security; diversity and wellbeing; human resources; marketing and PR (including social media); practitioners/teams and social cohesion; data security and information technology; space and facilities; and health and safety.

7. Conclusion

There is no one-size-fits-all, off-the-peg solution to risk assessment and emergency planning, and for it to have any value in a chambers it needs to involve people at every level and provide the opportunity for input and discussion. This in itself can be onerous and time consuming, but being open about some of the issues that need addressing is a surprisingly engaging approach. The effort involved must be proportionate to the perceived level of risk in chambers; in a successful cohesive set the risks may be minimal and good housekeeping is all that is required.

Risk assessment is a regulatory requirement, and in some instances a legal requirement, but this is not the prime reason for doing it. The legal profession is undergoing rapid change and the chambers that can anticipate problems and mitigate their effects will be stronger. The process of risk management also creates opportunities: opportunities to improve client care, identify options for business development and enhance a reputation. It can be seen as a key element of a chambers' strategic plan and can be utilised to test out proposed projects. How many times have chambers decided on exciting and innovative proposals without really investigating the risks? Even when the finances appear to add up, have all the indirect costs been considered? The time and effort of careful evaluation and planning are worth the investment because the cost of getting it wrong will always be much greater. The ability to remain competitive in a changing market is built on properly analysing and addressing risk.

Technology @ the Bar

Felicity Schneider
Littleton Chambers

1. Introduction

Whenever I mention that I work in a set of barristers' chambers, inevitably the first question people ask is whether the Bar resembles how it is portrayed in the BBC's legal television show *Silk*. Having never watched the series I am never able to comment; however, what this question does make me appreciate is that to the outside world the Bar and its inner workings appear to be wholly entrenched in the traditions and practices very consciously upheld and sustained since the days of Dickens. The wearing of long black gowns, stiff white collars and horse hair wigs in court, dressing in traditional silk breeches accompanied by a frilled white shirt and black, buckled patent leather shoes for silk ceremonies bears testimony to these bastions of tradition and protocol. In addition, his smooth blend of vast intellectual ability and persuasive eloquence remains the barrister's very unique domain of expertise. So, against this very traditional, longstanding and largely unchanged backdrop one might be curious to know if, how and to what degree modern technology has been embraced by and impacted on the Bar.

In this chapter I will endeavour to cover briefly the emergence of technology and its adoption within the legal environment where the Bar operates, moving on to review the basic structure of the Bar and why it generally presents such unique challenges, especially in relation to technology and its application. I will then seek to explore more recent technology advancements and developments, and how their proposed implementation will likely affect the legal sector and more specifically the Bar. Finally, I will look to future, prospective technology and how it might be applied or adopted by the Bar, concluding with some personal predictions which I believe will transpire within the forthcoming decade and how they will likely change the landscape of the Bar as we know it today.

2. The emergence of technology and its adoption at the Bar

Up until the early 1980s those who worked at the Bar, both barristers and staff, worked in much the same way they had for decades. Systems were exclusively manual and paper-rich, the bespoke craft of a barrister was time intensive and deeply intellectual, and the phrase 'inking the diary' held relevant meaning to those working at the Bar. Technology had yet to surface but was being developed, and it would ultimately change the face of the world, business and the Bar. Looking back at those days we can barely imagine working without some of the technologies which we now take for granted and upon which we are now so heavily reliant.

By around the mid-1980s technology made its first glimpses in the workplace and would, in due course, also appear at the Bar. Some initial technology included the first 'portable' computer, the Osborne, the word-processing package Lotus 1-2-3, Apple Inc's Macintosh 128K computer and the advent of the first mobile calls in the United Kingdom in 1985. The attraction of personal computers for those early adopters at the Bar was almost exclusively for their word processing capabilities. There were some progressive individuals at the Bar who, as early as the late 1980s and early 1990s, made regular use of bulletin boards such as Link, AOL (America Online) and Compu-Serve in the days pre-Internet and pre-email. By late 1991 the World Wide Web was opened as a public domain, having previously serviced only a small, select group within the scientific community and government employees as a means of sharing and exchanging data. This development would lead to the biggest explosion of knowledge the world would ever experience and, unsurprisingly, was closely followed by the launch of the very first search engines, Yahoo and Netscapes, in 1994. Although the first emails had successfully been sent by Ray Tomlinson as early as 1971, it was not until the Internet came of age around 1992 that email became more globally considered as a viable form of communication. Given its speed of delivery, email was soon to become the default form of communication within the legal sector, despite predictions to the contrary by the Solicitors Regulation Authority. In the early 1990s barristers' clerks made use of an online diary management system called ACE, but by 1993 most had graduated to Meridian Law, a bespoke software solution locally hosted, in a chambers' 'server room', which enabled clerks to manage barristers' diaries and retain critical case and client contact information, as well as process and record details relating to barristers' fees, generate fee notes and record fee payments electronically. This hosted service would prove to be absolutely central to the effective functioning of the Bar in the future.

By the mid-1990s most barristers had their own personal computers installed in chambers, which they used primarily for word processing, email communications and web browsing. Despite its seemingly ready adoption at the Bar, technology was only ever considered an enabler and, as Richard Susskind and Daniel Susskind observed:

> the assumption made by most professionals was that machines would prove to be handy tools... a sensible replacement for the filing cabinet, good at generating documents quickly, a splendid back-office resource.[1]

There remained a view that technology would fail in any meaningful way to impact or change the essential nature of the work undertaken at the Bar and, I believe, this view still prevails today to some significant degree.

In 2007 two important technologies appeared which would significantly impact the Bar. On 1 February 2007 Bar Squared launched LEX as an alternative diary management system to Meridian Law, which had dominated the sector since the mid-1990s. LEX was hugely innovative and fully supported the working practices of clerks, barristers and chambers. What set LEX above its software predecessors was

---

1   Richard Susskind & Daniel Susskind, *The Future of the Professions: How Technology will transform the work of Human Experts*, 2015.

that it is built on a .NET platform supported by Microsoft SQL databases and it uses a web browser as the client to ensure that it is both forwards and backwards compatible and can thus seamlessly incorporate future technologies. Since its inception LEX has been installed in over 200 sets across England and Wales and continues to achieve market dominance within this very niche marketplace. The diary management system continues to be the central hub at the Bar into which all cases, client information and records are stored, and it remains integral to the successful management and running of individual practices, cases and chambers.

The second technology innovation came later that same year, in June 2007, when Apple launched the first iPhone. This was the first-ever handheld device to fully integrate mobile communications, email and access to the Internet on one mobile platform and, as had been anticipated, it took the world by storm. Blair Janis, director of software & technology at Wealth Counsel, believes that "the release of the iPhone has arguably had more impact on how we have integrated the use of technology into our daily work and personal lives than any other technology".[2] This development ushered in an era of change and technological development at a pace never previously experienced, and the Bar was quick to embrace this new technology given that it fully enabled barristers to access important case and diary information, emails and documents, and stay in touch with their clerks while out of chambers. An unforeseen side effect of the introduction of the iPhone at the Bar was that Apple MAC hardware and software was quickly introduced into the chambers' server estate, which had until then been exclusively supporting a Microsoft Windows environment. This change would bring with it a unique set of challenges for the Bar.

3.   What makes the Bar so 'unique' from a technology perspective

So how, you may ask, does the Bar differ from other business or commercial organisations to which technology and technological advancements apply? Chambers is essentially a service company out of which a number of individual, self-employed barristers work and through which they collectively share the services provided by staff and overhead expenses. This means that chambers functions as a non-profit organisation. Many are registered as trade protection associations, although there has been a growing trend in more recent years for chambers to register as companies limited by guarantee. Chambers has no managing partner/s, no shareholders and no directors or board members.

Most chambers are democratically managed and run by an elected management committee, which takes overall responsibility for the effective and efficient governance of chambers; however, even in 2017, some chambers remain autocratic and are managed by a senior clerk and barrister or a senior clerk alone. For those democratically inclined organisations, the management of chambers is run in strict accordance with their Constitution, which outlines the obligations of barristers to chambers. The management committee is usually supported by many, smaller strategic committees which focus on specific areas relating to chambers, such as business development, information technology, finance and pupillage, to name a

---

2   http://americanbar.org/publications/gp-solo/2014/may-june.

few. These committees are mostly led by a combination of barristers and senior staff. A natural consequence of this 'run by committee' approach is that any proposed change takes an inordinately long time to be discussed, debated, agreed and implemented because, understandably, as self-employed individuals the priority of barristers is their professional work, which takes precedence over any committee obligations, regardless of how committed or dedicated they are to the function or purpose of said committee. Given that the recommendations of any committee would need to achieve approval of the management committee and subsequently be voted for by a majority of the membership before it can be formally adopted, it is not surprising that the fundamental structure of chambers goes some way to explain why the Bar lags behind in adopting technological advancements where others are more commercially agile and therefore earlier adopters.

In addition, since each barrister within a set of chambers is a self-employed practitioner, unique challenges are presented from a technology perspective. In other corporate organisations IT hardware, software, strategies and approaches are centrally determined and applied. At the Bar, however, where each barrister provides his own IT hardware and software and his own individually unique setup and working practices, very little uniformity of systems or approach can be easily achieved. The result is that any new technology solution/s need to be significantly flexible to accommodate these variables and often there is a need to run a number of parallel systems simultaneously in order to achieve a common outcome.

Finally, because of the very nature and fundamental structure of chambers, its annual investment in IT infrastructure and technology is considerably less than that of its commercial counterparts. Dependent of course on the size of chambers, it might invest only between 7% and 10% of its annual budget on IT infrastructure, the bulk of which pays for the provision of IT support services to its barristers and staff. When considering why the Bar demonstrates a limited ability to make strategic investment in technological change, Jitendra Valera of IRIS Legal summarises:

> the criteria used by Chambers to assess technology is often limited. Far too much emphasis is placed on the functionality needed right now, the cheapest price, the latest trend or gadget or because the Chambers 'down the road' has it.[3]

But these trends are changing and the more progressive and forward-thinking sets are now adopting a strategic approach where decisions and budgets, especially in relation to technology and its implementation, are more aligned with a vision of what and how technology can help chambers to compete and be more successful in the new legal world. Many now adopt a vision and culture which reflects their chambers as a 'business' and are "constantly monitoring ways in which they can win, retain and service clients, grow their income, be productive and save time and money".[4]

Over the past decade the Bar has continued to embrace and embed an ever-expanding spectrum of technological advancements within its arsenal. With

---

3   Jitendra Valera, 'How to Survive the 21st Century', *The Barrister*, www.barristermagazine.com/barrister/index.php?id=469.

4   *Ibid.*

significantly increased processing power and storage capacity of devices, connectivity expanding and speed improving, hardware becoming more affordable, computing becoming more portable and the ever-increasing move to cloud-based solutions, an unforeseen side effect which has taken hold over time is that barristers have fully embraced the opportunity to work flexibly, resulting in them physically coming into chambers less often. To some degree this has diminished the collegiate and collective environment which for so many years has been treasured and believed to be central to the success and uniqueness of the Bar.

In most organisations, advances in technology drive them to revisit their own business model and processes, and can therefore be a massive enabler. The Bar is not immune from this and some of the primary drivers of change at the Bar are pressures to drive down costs, government-driven transformation initiatives which focus on fair access to justice, and regulatory scrutiny and compliance.

Traditionally barristers have charged for their legal expertise and advice on a time-based system, but it is predicted that clients in future will be more inclined only to pay for the "value delivered rather than the effort expended".[5] This highlights the need for improved efficiencies at the Bar, and one possible means of achieving this would be to adopt appropriate technology to enhance and speed up output and productivity.

4. Modern technological innovation and advancement and its impact on the Bar

Government-driven legal initiatives in the United Kingdom have served particularly to address the issue of fair access to justice, since litigation is known to be very costly and therefore only accessible to the very rich, who are able to pay these high costs, or the very poor, via access to legal aid. Making the law more affordable and subsequently more accessible has proved to be a primary driver of change in the UK justice system. According to Bloomberg, "British commercial courtrooms have been slow to adopt technology"[6] and ex-Conservative Justice Secretary, Michael Gove, had complained in the past about the "antiquated ways of working, grotesque inefficiencies and snowdrifts of paper" he had witnessed clogging up the law courts.[7] To that end, a virtual court system (e-Courts) in England and Wales has been widely discussed as part of the Ministry of Justice's proposed new digital strategy. This implementation would certainly encompass e-disclosure and digitalised case processes and, of course, the success of this initiative will be subject to the courts being fully e-doc enabled. A budget of around £700 million was approved for this project in 2016 and is currently awaiting ratification by Parliament before being implemented. Singapore already has an Electronic Litigation System[8] in place, which it believes helps to achieve effective, efficient and economical dispensing and

5 Richard Susskind & Daniel Susskind, *The Future of the Professions: How Technology will transform the work of Human Experts*, 2015.
6 www.bloomberg.com/news/features/2017-05-23/the-exquitely-english-and-amazingly-lucrative-world-of-london-clerks.
7 www.ft.com/content.
8 http://supcourt.gov.sg.

administration of justice. In England and Wales CE File,[9] an electronic filing and case management system, was trialled in 2015 to enable professional court users who had previously filed documents in paper form and paid court fees manually to file documents electronically and pay court fees online. This system has now been successfully extended to all the jurisdictions of the Rolls Building and will likely expand to other courts in the years ahead. Legal technologists however are currently asking more profound questions about "whether Court is in fact a place or a service and whether there is any compelling need for people to congregate in physical courtrooms to settle disputes".[10] While the UK judiciary proposes that virtual court rooms (e-Courts) can be an effective alternative solution to current practices, it believes that effective online dispute resolution (ODR) presents yet another "exciting milestone" which could assist in achieving its overall aims.[11] In 2016 Lord Justice Briggs published his final report on the structure of civil courts, where he backed the development of ODR for civil disputes where the value of claims is less than £25,000, and he subsequently recommended to HM Courts & Tribunals Service that it establish an Internet-based court service, known as HM Online Court, where members of the judiciary would decide cases online and interact electronically with parties. The Bar will therefore need to plan ahead in order to adjust to such changes.

Technology and regulation almost always presents a chicken and egg scenario, with the introduction of new technology inevitably creating a shift which in turn creates a necessity for new regulation to be applied. This applies even more so at the Bar given the very nature of its work and it is for this reason that the legal sector remains highly regulated. Certainly, a spate of hefty fines levied by the Information Commissioner's Office on barristers and staff working at the Bar has helped to focus minds on regulation. The Bar Standards Board, which regulates barristers and the Bar in England and Wales, has in recent years applied more stringent regulation over technology and its application, thus driving home to individual practitioners their professional obligations and responsibilities as active users of technology. In order to ensure ongoing compliance of self-employed barristers at the Bar, many sets have introduced a comprehensive IT policy specifically focused on barristers, which outlines the various mandatory regulatory and compliance obligations with which they must comply. Despite some initial reluctance, such policies have now gained traction and this has resulted in improved compliance.

It cannot be ignored that a growing number of solicitor firms are increasingly looking to technology to leverage competitive advantage which enables them to streamline and automate their legal processes primarily to reduce costs. This fact is supported by the raft of innovation and evolving technology being developed within the legal sector, and as solicitor firms readily embrace these new technologies and working practices the Bar will be pressured to follow.

One of the final elements driving change within the legal sector is the

9   www.ce-file.uk.
10   Richard Susskind & Daniel Susskind, *The Future of the Professions: How Technology will transform the work of Human Experts*, 2015.
11   www.judiciary.gov.uk/wp-content/uploads/2015/02/Online-Dispute-Resolution-Find_Web-Version1.pdf.

introduction of alternative business structures (ABSs). With much of the initial hype about how these new non-legal non-traditional entities would enter and dominate the legal domain now having dissipated given that take up has been relatively low, the establishment of these new entities cannot be ignored. A number of large firms, such as the "Big 4" accounting firms and others, have registered ABSs and it is clear that their intention is to ultimately encroach on the legal turf traditionally associated with the Bar; this will inevitably alter the way in which legal services are structured and delivered. While the introduction of these new entities will not necessarily affect in any significant way the many practitioners who already have established, illustrious careers at the Bar nor those who continue to represent high-profile, high-complexity, high-value cases, those in 2017 who seek a traditional career trajectory at the Bar will likely discover that the Bar of tomorrow will be quite different from the way it is structured and works today. So how is the legal landscape changing and what developments in technology will likely change the work of those at the Bar?

In 2017, significant advancements in ODR technologies are appearing online, many of which purport to provide more cost-effective legal services. Some of the major players include Ajuve, Modria (in the United States) and the EU ODR platform Mediate. Ajuve[12] is a low-cost online system that takes users through every stage of a dispute from making a complaint to resolution and making a binding award via an independent arbitrator, which it delivers in no more than six weeks. Fees charged for this service are agreed up front and based on the amount in dispute. Modria[13] was developed by the co-founders of the ODR systems developed specifically for eBay and PayPal; bearing in mind eBay's bespoke ODR system handles approximately 60 million disputes among its traders each year, this option provides a very compelling argument. Associated Press heralds these systems as: "the next wave of technology in which the law is turned into computer code that can solve legal battles without the need for a judge or attorney". Mediate[14] is an online mediation portal encompassing its tagline 'everything mediation'.

More recently developed technologies, which are more specifically focused on the offerings of the Bar, include online portal Clerksroom,[15] which claims: "You need legal help. We aim to make that simple", and puts members of the public in touch with a barrister who can help them with their case, and MyBarrister,[16] which helps direct access clients locate a suitable barrister to instruct. While it is noted that these two latter technologies do not replace the actual services a barrister provides but rather connect clients and barristers, FromCounsel[17] provides a more all-encompassing service. Launched in the United Kingdom in December 2016, it is supported by 22 barristers from Erskine Chambers and "provides authoritative commentary and analysis on English corporate law through an innovative technology platform". It purports to harness the collective knowledge of some of the

---

12   https://ajuve.com.
13   http://modria.com.
14   www.mediate.com/articles/euodr.cfm.
15   www.clerksroom.com.
16   www.mybarrister.co.uk.
17   www.fromcounsel.com.

leading barristers and professional support lawyers within this portal and the service is provided online via a subscription basis only. Some of FromCounsel's subscribers include the biggest Magic Circle law firms in the United Kingdom. AbsoluteBarrister[18] supplies unbundled barrister legal services online for a fixed fee, agreed in advance. For those not entirely convinced of the usefulness or effectiveness of such an integrated online service offering, you might be tempted to read through some of their client reviews.[19] TrialPad[20] is currently one of the most expensive legal apps available but one of the best designed and the top selling. It works in conjunction with apps such as Dropbox and is considered the ultimate when it comes to document management and trial preparation. Another is Riverview Law,[21] incorporating Riverview Chambers, which is a DLA Piper initiative where lawyers and barristers work collaboratively via an online platform to provide legal services. Opus 2 Magnum™[22] is a more recent arrival and, according to its website, is:

the only worldwide legal services company that blends sophisticated "cloud" technology with court reporting excellence to modernise evidence management during high-stakes matters across the globe – including litigation, arbitration hearings and government inquiries.

It is considered a fast and nimble virtual data room that mimics how litigation professionals work on paper. The highly collaborative environment enables document sharing, notation on documents (which can be private or shared), hyperlinks between documents, idea shares, individual task management, monitoring of progress, instant messaging between team members and court automated transcription, which provides real-time transcription of court proceedings allowing for call up of relevant documents referred to by the judge when required, as well as logging a comprehensive activity/audit history on the system. As such, it "redefines how sensitive information is accessed, reviewed and shared during 21st century transactions".[23] This platform provides legal professionals and the courts with an effective, integrated paperless option spanning document disclosure, case preparation and presentation. This innovative technology promises a seamless, cross-party and fully collaborative environment which fully complements and supports the work of legal professionals. Some silks from Littleton Chambers who have recently used this system have found it to be very impressive and believe that in future years its use by the Bar will continue to gain traction and become more widespread.

However, it is clear that although a vast array of innovative technologies are being developed and filtering into various sectors of the legal domain, these remain predominantly enabling technologies in that they provide assistance or improved methodology options. This demonstrates, without doubt, that at this time technology will not replace legal minds and therefore the very bespoke realm of the oral advocate will remain unchanged for the foreseeable future. However, will this

---

18 www.absolutebarrister.com.
19 www.absolutebarrister.com/reviews.
20 www.litsoftware.com/trialpad.
21 www.riverviewlaw.com.
22 www.opus2.com.
23 www.opus2.com/forum.

change with the huge advances being made in artificial intelligence (AI) and cognitive machine learning?

It is an accepted fact that the legal sector is one which has not yet been radically transformed by the technology revolution, despite such advancements providing many real benefits and useful implementation tools to assist lawyers with their documentation presentation or review processes. Where work at the Bar remains profoundly intellectual, practitioners remain sceptical, even reluctant, to consider that innovative technology could potentially analyse legal situations and leverage viable solutions to largely complex legal problems. Fabian Horton, owner of Australian Connect Law, believes that "[L]aw at its core is information and the application of that information".[24] Working on that premise, many legal technology companies have in recent years been exploring the extent to which "the cognitive domain of legal experts can be automated by applying AI (Artificial Intelligence) to legal problems and tasks to improve efficiency, accuracy and save time".[25] Building on such cognitive machine technology, in October 2016 three Cambridge University students launched LawBot,[26] which is acclaimed to be "the world's most advanced legal chatbot"[27] helping users determine, through a series of intuitive oral questions, if they have been a victim of crime and providing advice on how they might seek assistance. LawBot, considered to constitute an 'artificial lawyer', provides empathetic responses to users, resulting in no two conversations with users being the same. The development team are currently teaching LawBot 'emotions', so that by recognising users' emotional states it will be able to respond to them with compassion and sensitivity.

5.   The future of technology at the Bar

The biggest and most significant technological advancements predicted to bring waves of dramatic change in the way we live and work over the next 20 years are in the arena of 'big data', where high-processing capacity machines are used to discern patterns and correlations, identify trends and offer insights and accurate predictions previously never conceived of. In *The Future of the Professions*, Richard Susskind and Daniel Susskind believe that these machine predictions "will often draw conclusions, offer advice and provide guidance at the standard of human experts or higher".[28] One such cognitive computer system is IBM's Watson,[29] which has the capacity to perform complex analytics on huge volumes of unstructured data. Watson's primary focus is to collate data from various sources, which it interprets to expose language patterns, connections and insights, and then organises the information into usable content. Cognitive systems such as Watson learn from how humans interact with them and so continually refine their actions and responses. Another is ROSS,[30] a digital legal

---

24   www.collaw.edu.au.
25   'The Future of Legal Services', The Law Society of England and Wales, January 2016.
26   www.lawbot.info.
27   www.barristermagazine.com/trends-in-legal-technology-the-art-of-the-possible/.
28   Richard Susskind & Daniel Susskind, *The Future of the Professions: How Technology will transform the work of Human Experts*, 2015.
29   www.ibm.com/smartphone/us/en/ibmwatson.
30   www.rossintelligence.com.

expert which continually monitors the law via topical documentation, including legislation, case law, statutes, books and secondary sources such as online articles, blogs and all forms of social media to advise legal professionals of recent legal outcomes. ROSS mines vast collections of legal data, analyses the legal information and provides precise and appropriate responses to complicated legal questions. Given that legal professionals rely on a combination of their formal knowledge, experience and skills to undertake their work and the repeated recycling of such acquired knowledge enables them to achieve success, imagine for a moment how this process might be even more significantly enhanced by using a super-cognitive machine to quickly assimilate the ever-growing bodies of legal knowledge to provide practitioners at the Bar with quick and accurate diagnostics of the relevant data. While prior to the advent of the Internet we regularly complained about the lack of sufficient information upon which to base our decisions, we are now suffering at the other end of the spectrum from information overload, so the benefit to legal practitioners would be in harnessing technology to intelligently sift through and determine the relevant legal information contained within the copious quantity of data currently available, often referred to as 'big data'.

We know that practical legal expertise and knowledge has historically been held in people's heads, libraries, textbooks and filing cabinets, but increasingly this expertise is being stored and represented in digital format in a variety of high-capacity, maximum processing power machines, systems, applications and tools, and being handled, shared, used and re-used in very different ways. This is borne out by the exponential increase in volume of strategic market intelligence being made available by legal publishers Lexis Nexis and Westlaw, and it would therefore be no great surprise if our first glimpse of the merging of legal intelligence and cognitive computing is proffered by these providers. While practitioners at the Bar have generally embraced the use of legal information portals to access relevant information, few have any clear idea about how future, innovative technologies might further enable them to enhance their legal output.

Understandably there remains a reluctance at the Bar to acknowledge that machines, with their rapid advancement capabilities and enhanced AI machine learning, will in time come to be accepted as trusted partners working closely in tandem alongside the legal professionals of tomorrow. This might be the case because the burning question and most hotly debated topic within the legal sector currently is: "What happens when machines get it wrong?" This ethical dilemma will continue to prevail until we have satisfactory answers and therefore the technology will, in all likelihood, be held sufficiently at bay. However, what is important is that even though barristers will unlikely be early adopters who work at the 'bleeding edge' of technology, it is recommended that they endeavour to keep abreast of technological advancements and strive to become more adept and agile users of technology as this will better equip them to deal with future advances and developments.

For many who were working pre-technology careers in the mid-1980s, myself included, we could never have imagined or believed that within the next 25 years advances in technology would have resulted in such deep and profound changes in our personal and professional lives, to the extent that in 2017 we can hardly imagine a life without, to name a few, broadband, the Internet, email, mobile phones, Facebook, Twitter, Skype, Amazon, online banking, apps, bitcoins and Google. The technology revolution has long since begun and will continue to build momentum over the forthcoming decades. We can easily be forgiven if we are unable to foresee with any degree of clarity or comprehend where and how technology may take us and how this will affect professional lives of those at the Bar over the next two decades.

While some of the technological advancements might possibly sound just a little too far-fetched, perhaps a few of the Top 25 Technology Predictions as made by Dave Evans, chief futurist of Cisco might help to focus the mind on the extent to which technology is far reaching. He predicts that by 2020 a $1,000 PC will have the raw processing power of a human brain. By 2030 it will take a village of human brains to match the processing power of the same PC, and that by 2050, assuming a global population of 9 billion, the same value PC will equal the processing power of all human brains on the earth.[31] In addition, while a human speed reader can read around 100 to 150 pages of information per hour, IBM's Watson accesses 80 teraflops (a trillion floating-point operations or 10^{12} units of information) per second and ROSS mines data from about one billion text documents in less than three seconds. It would seem remiss of anyone, least of all those at the Bar, not to be alive to how these developments might trigger a sustained period of disruption and realignment of services within the legal sector.

While I am no legal technologist, I have worked at the Bar for over 12 years and have always had a very keen interest in technology as an enabler and facilitator, and I do believe that within the next decade working practices at the Bar will change as a result of technological advancement and adoption, in the following ways:

- Oral advocacy as currently practised at the Bar will remain mostly immune to being overtaken or replaced by technology. However, there will be a greater adoption of enabling technologies which will complement and support the work of those practising at the Bar. Moves towards paperless practices, use of digital collaboration forums and the initial, although limited use, of cognitive machines to assist with legal data collection, review and assimilation will become more readily adopted as these technologies mature.
- The increased adoption of technology at the Bar will likely result in the increase of more non-traditional employees employed in more non-traditional legal roles in the future. While some currently functional employee roles will in all likelihood become redundant, given the clear move towards digital systems such as e-filing and e-courts, a raft of new employee roles will evolve within the sector. These might include legal project managers, legal technologists and technology facilitators.
- General legal practice will diminish in time given the trend towards commoditisation of the law. As this comes to bear on the Bar, I believe successful practitioners will evolve to become experts in very narrow and

very specific areas of the law, much like orthopaedic surgeons now prefer to be classified as specialist 'hand' or 'knee' surgeons. Those who achieve expert, niche practices will continue to sustain their relevance in a competitive marketplace and their professional lifespan will endure.

- The traditional chambers model that has for so long characterised, served and serviced the Bar will likely become redundant, with large sets fracturing into smaller sets given the move of practitioners towards specialised, niche areas of legal expertise. Contrary to the current trend that 'bigger is better', the commercial agility afforded smaller specialist sets will better suit them to navigate and adapt to the new legal landscape as it emerges in order to take advantage of the many new opportunities such will present. As technology continues to enable and facilitate effective remote working, the retention of large, costly buildings for chambers will become redundant. Unfortunately, the most profound impact of this will be the dissolution of the traditional collegiate nature of the Bar which has been so long established and respected.

- ABSs will continue to encroach into the legal sector. The fact that the Big 4 accounting firms and other large organisations have already registered ABSs clearly indicates their future intentions. While the services these organisations ultimately set up may not directly impact those working at the Bar, what they will achieve is the driving down of legal costs and the capture of a portion of market share that was previously the exclusive domain of the Bar. To that end barristers will need to remain acutely aware of how these changes affect their overall business strategy and approach of chambers and its practitioners.

- While many sets currently have business plans or a strategic roadmap which outlines the short- to medium-term goals and objectives of chambers, its practitioners and staff, there are many that do not. For those that do not, I would strongly recommend these plans be put in place as they will enable chambers to outline and develop a clear vision of the challenges and opportunities that lie ahead and how these might best be exploited or overcome. Emerging technology must of course be an essential inclusion in this plan.

By its very nature, the Bar is, and always has been, generally risk averse and change is neither readily nor easily embraced. While we may as individuals and organisations be afraid of change and the uncertainty and disruption it might ultimately bring, we cannot deny that the wheels of the technology revolution have already begun to turn and will only continue to accelerate in the years ahead. Our best defence will be to keep informed, remain agile and embrace the coming change. The Bar should continue to focus on the opportunities these changes might present, given, as Yuval Noah Harari so aptly proclaims, "the single greatest constant of history is that everything changes".[32]

---

32   Yuval Noah Harari, *Homo Deus: A Brief History of Tomorrow*, 2015.

Pro bono/CSR

Chris Broom
Gray's Inn Tax Chambers

1. Introduction

In 1980 when I started my career as a barristers' clerk, *pro bono* and corporate social responsibility (CSR) were not something that the Bar championed in the way it has been seen to embrace them today. Since its inception, the Bar, as a profession, has always, without fail, shown acts of kindness to people in need, but until more recently this was on a case-by-case basis rather than through any organised structure. Then, it was still very early days for some of the legal charities that we know today and some were yet to be born.

1.1 Pro bono

I remember Robin Soule, my first senior clerk, telling me that Anthony Scrivener QC was appearing in a case *pro bono* and me not having any real understanding of what the term actually meant. Robin explained that it was:

> *free legal advice or representation provided by lawyers to individuals and or community groups who cannot afford to pay for that advice or representation and where public funding is not available.*

I have tidied that up considerably from what he actually said to me at the time as my mother may read this chapter. Robin did not suffer fools gladly, like most of the senior clerks with whom my generation started our careers. How times have changed. Back then you did not look at *pro bono* in business terms. While it was always a good thing to help your fellow man (person), you certainly did not think of it as part of your business model or that it may give you or your chambers a possible advantage over the competition.

I strongly believe (as many people in the profession do) that every person should have the right to access justice no matter what their financial circumstances are. Unfortunately, with government cutbacks to legal aid (whichever party is in power), the Bar has had to step forward and do even more work for free – a large proportion of which would have previously been paid for by legal aid. Some may argue that if the Bar did not take this view, the Government would have to tackle the legal aid problem. We could debate that point for many an hour, but that would not assist the many thousands of people helped by acts of kindness from the Bar at all levels every day, and this chapter would be longer than the whole of this fine publication.

The continuing generosity of the Bar makes me immensely proud as a senior clerk, and to be part of the system that makes this happen brings its own reward. I know many of my colleagues in practice management feel exactly the same way and do whatever they can to assist and encourage working pupils and members of their chambers and staff teams to all get involved in *pro bono* and CSR activities.

1.2   CSR

Collins English Dictionary defines 'corporate social responsibility' as "the incorporation of ethical elements, such as the public interest and environmental concern, into the planning of business strategy". But what does CSR mean to a member of the Bar today? Well, it can mean so many things, so let us take a look at just a few of the ways a modern set of chambers approaches its CSR. Chambers, as we know them, are a collection of individuals practising under the same roof sharing (mostly) the same ideals, so to marshal any individual barrister or chambers into working for free or looking at their CSR may or may not take some convincing. With that being said, the positive long-term effect on a barrister's practice proves the point time and time again and it is without doubt an essential part of a proper business model to consider right from the start of pupillage all the way through taking silk (becoming a Queen's Counsel).

Business development is something we all do every single day as clerks/practice managers, and we must always have one eye open for profile-raising opportunities for the individual barrister/barrister teams or chambers as a whole. CSR and *pro bono* give you that opportunity if you are prepared to make the effort.

A CSR business model in chambers usually consists of actions that further some social good beyond the interests of those chambers and involves all members of chambers, pupils and staff. Examples of the CSR initiatives that have been set up by different chambers in recent years include volunteering within the local community, providing both financial and educational support for local schools, and encouraging a work experience placement in chambers to enthuse people from diverse backgrounds to develop a career at the Bar. Certain chambers also have an arrangement to assist in local law centres. A number of chambers have made *pro bono*/CSR initiatives part of their constitutions, so that when you join chambers you know what is expected of you right from the start and it is considered part of your career development within chambers. However, not all sets of chambers are the same so you may find yourself in a set that may require you to make your own way along the *pro bono*/CSR path. You should not be afraid to explore what you can do as an individual, engage with your clerk/practice manager and try and enthuse your fellow members of chambers and staff team as a whole to get on board with any ideas you may have.

2.   Legal charities and initiatives

Your clerk/practice manager will know of the many legal charities and be able to advise you of the one or even several that best suit your practice area – or even those outside of your usual practice area if you are feeling that you can bring benefit. To try and assist you in that process I have listed a number of the legal support charities and initiatives (but by all means not all) that you are likely to come across starting at the Bar – you may possibly already have colleagues in chambers working with such initiatives and your clerk/practice manager may well have contacts there with whom you can connect.

2.1   Bar *Pro Bono* Unit

Let us start with the Bar *Pro Bono* Unit (BPBU), which covers England and Wales. Some say the unit is the jewel in the crown of the Bar. I must confess at this point to being a trustee of the BPBU so I may show a little bias, but for good reason. It never ceases to amaze me the commitment and support the unit is given by members of the Bar, the specialist bar associations, the Bar Council, the various Inns of Court, the judiciary and also the clerks/practice managers and support staff in chambers. I would also like to take this opportunity to mention and thank the team who manage and run the unit who, as do all the staff teams of all the legal charities and initiatives, work incredibly hard with ever-increasing workloads and are rarely mentioned unsung heroes.

Every chairman of the Bar (since Peter Goldsmith QC) has made *pro bono* work the number one priority in their agenda, with the BPBU at the forefront of this initiative. Formed in 1996 by a group of barristers led by Peter Goldsmith QC (now Lord Peter Goldsmith QC and President of the BPBU) with 300 volunteer barristers receiving on average 30 cases a month, it has grown today to 3,750 volunteer barristers on the panel with over 2,169 (and rising) applications for help received every year. The unit is the only *pro bono* charity to provide access to legal assistance in nearly every area of law in all courts and tribunals, receiving cases from over 700 referral agencies from across England and Wales. The unit is an application-based service which can be accessed via referral from advice agencies, law centres, the Citizen's Advice Bureau, law clinics, solicitors, barristers and the member of public's local MP. Once the application is logged and a member of staff at the unit has checked the papers, they are sent to a senior barrister (a reviewer) to be reviewed. If rejected, the reasons why are explained to the applicant, but if accepted, the process begins of searching for a barrister volunteer to take the matter on. This is where you come in as that volunteer who looks at the matter to see if you can help. It may be that your clerk/practice manager has brought the matter to you or that you have seen the case offered on the BPBU website. At an early stage of your Bar career you will find this invaluable training and it will help you build your confidence and make you a better lawyer in the process. Ask any clerk/practice manager: the more experience you have at the start of your career, whether in court or advisory work, the better lawyer you have the potential to be; and to be able to mix this with your fee-paying work will make your practice mature much faster. Not only that but your shop window to the world – your chambers' website – will start to look more impressive not only by you advertising the fact that you do *pro bono* work, but by the list of recent cases you have appeared in growing by the week. A recent online discussion mentioned that 80% of leading law firms were more impressed by CVs showing evidence of *pro bono* work on a barrister's profile – something to be noted. More important than any of this is the life-changing results for so many people that you will hopefully make possible by your ongoing CSR and *pro bono* commitment right from the start of your career, continuing to when you take silk and become Queen's Counsel.

It should be noted that if you are practising at the Scottish or Northern Ireland Bar, the arrangements for your Bar *pro bono* work are slightly different. For Scotland, you will need to contact the Free Legal Services Unit at the Faculty of Advocates where you can volunteer your services[1] and for Northern Ireland, you will need to go through the Bar of Northern Ireland.[2]

2.2 Free Representation Unit

The Free Representation Unit (FRU) has recently celebrated its 45th birthday and has traditionally been aimed at attracting law students and legal professionals starting off their careers to provide legal advice, case preparation and advocacy in employment, social security and some criminal injury compensation tribunal cases being heard with a hearing date at a tribunal in London and the South East (or Nottingham). The FRU looks to train its volunteers and they are expected to visit the FRU office regularly while running cases. According to the latest figures released from the FRU, at any given time there are approximately 270 volunteer representatives working free of charge on behalf of the FRU. Many a young member of the Bar has had his first case appearing on behalf of a member of the public who has come to him via the FRU; its importance in the *pro bono* world cannot be overemphasised.

2.3 Bar associations

Equally, the various specialist bar associations have looked at how their members can help in whatever way possible with *pro bono* activities. One of the busiest schemes is CLIPS (Chancery Litigant in Person Support Scheme), which was set up in 2014 by the Chancery Bar Association as the brainchild of Lord Justice Briggs. This involves a duty system of barristers to help litigants in person appearing in the Interim Applications Court in the Chancery Division (Royal Courts of Justice) and the Central London County Court (CLCC). Barristers put their name down to volunteer via the Royal Courts of Justice Advice Bureau, promise to attend court (or be close to court) on a certain day, are placed on the rota and are expected to make themselves available to attend court if required. The scheme has been very successful and has attracted considerable attention among clerks/practice managers, who look at this as a way of getting their members of chambers in front of high court judges – more often usually when applying to become Queen's Counsel to bolster their judicial referees needed in the application for silk process. Some may raise an eyebrow at this reasoning, but one has to acknowledge the demands of the new business environment for the Bar and the need for clerks/practice managers to manage the careers of their principals and look for any opportunity to advance the career path of their members.

CLIPS is just one of many schemes that have been set up (or are in the process of being set up) by the various specialist bar associations, so when you join your chambers speak to your clerk/practice manager to see what connections your chambers has with the association close to the chambers' practice areas and get involved. If you find there is no connection, then become that person who makes that first connection and encourage your fellow members of chambers and staff team to all get involved. The same applies if you find there is no connection to the FRU

---

1   www.advocates.org.uk/instructing-advocates/free-legal-services-unit.
2   www.barofni.com/page/helping-the-community.

and the BPBU – reach out to them and they will be delighted to give you as much encouragement and support as they can to get you on board as a volunteer and/or as a chambers ambassador on their behalf.

2.4 *Pro Bono* Connect

Someone who did this is Jamie Goldsmith, barrister of One Essex Court with *Pro Bono* Connect. This has the benefit of two sides of the legal profession, the Bar and solicitors, coming together to support each other on *pro bono* matters. The scheme allows barristers from participating chambers doing *pro bono* cases to ask for solicitor assistance from a firm signed up to the scheme. One of the obvious benefits of this from a practice development point of view is the exposure to solicitors who you may not usually come across in the early part of your career, especially quite often those from Magic Circle firms, many of whom are signed up to this scheme.

2.5 Access to Justice Foundation

Another thing you can consider when appearing in a *pro bono* case is the costs position. When you have appeared in your *pro bono* case and have won on behalf of your client, you can ask the court to award *pro bono* costs which will find their way to another legal charity close to the Bar, the Access to Justice Foundation.

Pro bono costs orders are like ordinary costs orders, which can be claimed in civil proceedings where the successful party benefited from free legal advice or representation, whether for all or part of their case. Under Section 194 of the Legal Services Act 2007 you can claim the cost of any *pro bono* work you undertake on a civil case (even where some or the majority of the case was done on a fee-paying basis) from the paying party with an order in favour of the Access to Justice Foundation. The funding, which they collect (including via your costs awarded), is distributed to *pro bono* organisations, law centres and the Citizens Advice Bureau.

The Access to Justice Foundation aims to improve access to justice for the most vulnerable by funding organisations which provide legal advice and representation to those who need it the most. The foundation works with and supports a network of seven Legal Support Trusts that cover England and Wales to fund and support local free legal advice agencies which help to facilitate access to justice for the poorest, most vulnerable and most disadvantaged members of society.

The Legal Support Trusts raise funds primarily by organising sponsored events such as 'Legal Walks', as well as participating in national fundraising events. Last year the Trusts collectively raised over £1 million for free legal advice services, helping to enable access to justice nationwide. The London Legal Walk recently broke records for its 10th anniversary by raising over £560,000 and having 8,500 legal professionals participate. The walk is an ideal way to promote yourself and your chambers by entering a team and collecting sponsorship. Because it is so heavily attended by solicitors and in-house legal departments, this is an ideal way to make relationships with potential professional clients in a social environment, and many a brief has been picked up by clerks/practice managers as a direct result of involvement with the event. It should also be noted that it carries with it a huge social media presence, which can be taken advantage of to raise your individual or chambers' CSR profile on social media.

2.6   **Bar in the Community**

Bar in the Community is another CSR opportunity to consider. This gives charities the chance to find legally qualified trustees to join their boards via its website.[3] The website puts charities in contact with the Bar and allows members of the Bar to apply for trusteeship vacancies directly online. Being a trustee is a rewarding role and usually introduces you to the wider community at an earlier stage in your career.

3.   **Benefits of *pro bono*/CSR**

What I have discussed above should give you some practical ideas to consider as part of your business model, but how can all of this benefit you personally in terms of your *pro bono*/CSR work and act as a practical marketing tool to give you the edge over the competition?

Well, all clerks/practice managers have seen what works (and more importantly what does not) to promote and build a successful practice at an early stage or even later. Bear in mind that when I started as a junior clerk there were only 4,000 practising members of the Bar; there are now (at the last count) approximately 16,000 members of the Bar, very often chasing the same pieces of work from the same clients. That is a lot of competition.

You need to be thinking as early as your second six months of pupillage what your business plan is and discussing ideas with everyone around you. It is a bit like opening up a new sweet shop in the high street in town: why are people going to visit your shop and buy your sweets rather than the sweets from down the road or, more scarily, the next room to where you are sitting?

This may all sound a bit daft but think about it for a moment and you soon see the relevance. Your clerk/practice manager will have a much easier time offering your services (sweets) to prospective clients if you already have court and advisory experience under your belt, so *pro bono* work is to be snapped up to assist in being recognised for future fee-paying work.

You can also use the fact that you do *pro bono* work as a means of self-promotion by including it on your profile on chambers' website, as well as your LinkedIn profile and even your Twitter account – subject to the golden rule clerks/practice managers always say about Twitter: "read your tweet three times before you press send, or it may come back to haunt you".

Professional and lay clients are always impressed by seeing that the member of the Bar or chambers they are instructing has a social conscience and sometimes work for no reward. Like all of us these days, clients will make use of search engines to make informed decisions on their legal representatives, so the more times your name appears in their searches, the better. Some professional clients (eg, local authority departments) are required to put certain work out to tender every time they have the need to instruct a barrister, rather than just instructing a specific barrister/chambers which they may regularly use, so in the tendering process, questions are often asked about what the chambers/members do for their *pro bono*/CSR commitment. If you are unable to show such commitment, the work will more than likely go to the

---

3   www.barinthecommunity.org.uk.

competition that can; another reason to make *pro bono*/CSR an essential part of your business model.

3.1 Schemes

There are a number of schemes listed on the Bar Council's website that are available to barristers in England and Wales (some of which we have already touched on), which I have included below to point you in the right direction.[4] If there is nothing on the list below that you feel is for you, now is the time for you to be a pioneer and create a new one that does.

- The Bar *Pro Bono* Unit (BPBU): a national charity to facilitate the Bar's *pro bono* efforts for third six pupils, juniors and silks.
- The Free Representation Unit (FRU): student and junior barristers providing advocacy in tribunals mostly in employment and social security areas of law.
- The Bristol Family Law Scheme: for barristers mostly but open to solicitors to assist in family work at the Bristol Family Court.
- Chancery Bar Litigant in Person Support Scheme (CLIPS): members of the Chancery Bar Association, the Commercial Bar Association, the Technology and Construction Bar Association or the Employment Law Bar Association, or a solicitor advocate, volunteer for a day on a rota to provide advice and representation to litigants in person in the chancery applications list for interim applications in the chancery division in London Court 10, Rolls Building and also Central London County Court, Royal Courts of Justice.
- The Court 37 scheme for interim applications in the Queen's Bench Division, London.
- Employment Appeal Representation Service Scheme (EARS): set up to assist litigants in person before the Employment Appeal Tribunal (EAT).
- Employment Lawyers Appeals Advice Scheme (ELAAS): once a litigant in person has submitted their Rule 3(10) bundle to the EAT, they will be identified as unrepresented by the EAT and provided with an ELAAS volunteer to provide advice on the day of the hearing and assist with the hearing (where the advice is positive).
- Employment Appeal Tribunal Scheme (EAT): where an appellant has been successful at a Rule 3(10) at the EAT with the help of a representative acting under ELAAS, the ELAAS volunteer may then refer the case to the FRU or the BPBU.
- Employment Lawyers' Association 100 Days Project (ELA): where a piece of solicitor's work is suitable, the unit's caseworker should check if the applicant has given consent and if so, email the ELA with an anonymised summary outlining the piece of work required. If an ELA volunteer is available, the unit will then be informed.
- Employment Tribunal Litigant in Person Scheme (ELIPS): the scheme provides on-the-day advice to unrepresented litigants (claimants and respondents), aimed at those who cannot afford representation at the London Central Employment Tribunal.

---

4   With grateful thanks to the Bar Council of England & Wales.

- Court of Appeal scheme: these are cases that have been granted permission to appeal to the Court of Appeal and have been referred to the unit by the Royal Courts of Justice Advice Bureau.
- Court of Appeal Permissions scheme: these are cases that have been granted an oral hearing to ask for permission to appeal to the Court of Appeal.
- Inns' Disciplinary Scheme: the Inns' Scheme exists to enable Inn students with disciplinary issues to gain assistance from barristers through representation at hearings.
- Joint CILEX Bar Scheme (JIB): the CILEX *Pro Bono* Forum has a joint *pro bono* scheme with the BPBU. The scheme, JIB, allocates a suitable CILEX Fellow volunteer to work alongside a BPBU barrister, providing the services needed for the case.
- Personal Insolvency Litigation Advice & Representation Scheme (PILARS): these cases are sent to the unit's caseworkers from the Royal Courts of Justice Advice Bureau on a PILARS application form for defending a bankruptcy petition, applying to set aside a statutory demand or applying to annul a bankruptcy.
- Central London Family Court Scheme: ten family chambers near to the central London family court will send an advocate as and when is needed, with a day's notice.
- Cardiff Court Family Free Advice Clinic: operates from the Cardiff family court, providing legal advice, information and advocacy two days a week and is a collaboration between barristers, law firms and others.

Pro Bono Connect Network: a network of chambers and law firms willing to work together on *pro bono* cases, enabling a barrister from a participating set to request assistance from a participating solicitor (and vice versa). Barristers act through the BPBU.

3.2 International exposure

You may also consider increasing your international CSR/*pro bono* exposure. One of the most well-known associations you can join as a member of the Bar is the International Bar Association (IBA). The IBA is the world's leading organisation of international legal practitioners, Bar associations and law societies, with a membership of more than 80,000 lawyers and over 190 bar associations and law societies in 160 countries. It has considerable expertise in providing assistance to the global legal community. As I write this, its current conference is taking place in Sydney, Australia with UK Bar and clerks/practice managers represented; and with the IBA's many international *pro bono* projects being discussed, the exposure to international firms at all levels is invaluable and enables you to access worldwide lawyers' firms at a much earlier stage of your career path. As the Bar Council website notes:

> *The recognised expertise of barristers in advocacy means that their services are in high demand in the international legal market. In addition, parties frequently choose English law as the law under which to resolve disputes arising from international contracts, even*

though the subject matter and the parties may have no other connection with the jurisdiction of England and Wales. The popularity of English law, together with the experience gained by barristers in various international dispute forums, means that English barristers can offer clients from across the world considerable expertise in international dispute resolution.[5]

The strength of the Bar has always been its ability to adapt to the market place and embrace change. International work for most chambers is one of the growing areas of their marketing strategy and it is necessary to introduce members of chambers to worldwide firms at a much earlier stage of their career than perhaps was contemplated in the past – not only by the usual means, but also by considering involvement in *pro bono*/CSR initiatives relevant to the jurisdictions and their specific needs.

3.3   Volunteering

You could also consider expressing your CSR responsibilities by volunteering in areas with which you may feel a connection, whether that be political, social or academic, and giving them the benefit of your knowledge from being at the Bar. The list below is just a few of the organisations which would be very pleased to see you as a volunteer:[6]

- Advocacy Training Council (International Committee) www.advocacytrainingcouncil.org/international-work/introduction
- Advocates for International Development www.a4id.org
- Aire Centre www.airecentre.org
- Amnesty International www.amnesty.org.uk
- Bar Human Rights Committee www.barhumanrights.org.uk
- Beyond Borders Scotland www.beyondbordersscotland.com
- British Council www.britishcouncil.org
- Commonwealth Lawyers Association www.commonwealthlawyers.com
- Criminal Bar Association www.criminalbar.com
- European Human Rights Advocacy Centre www.ehrac.org.uk
- Fair Trials International www.fairtrials.org
- Friends of the Earth www.foe.co.uk
- Greenpeace www.greenpeace.org.uk
- Human Rights Lawyers Association www.hrla.org.uk
- Interights www.interights.org/home/index.html
- International Bar Association Human Rights www.ibanet.org/IBAHRI.aspx
- International Commission of Jurists www.icj.org

4.   Conclusion

I hope by now you are in agreement that making *pro bono*/CSR part of your overall business model can only be to your advantage when it comes to advancing your long-term career at the Bar. The final thought I wish to leave you with is how

---

5   www.barcouncil.org.uk/media/168701/barristers_in_the_international_legal_market_2012.pdf.
6   Again, grateful thanks to the Bar Council.

important it is to listen to your clerk/practice manager and/or colleagues in chambers and embrace any advice they may give you which has been built up through years of experience and seeing what works and what does not. Equally, I take the view that I will never stop learning as a senior clerk, so if someone who is just starting their career at the Bar comes to me with a new idea, and it is a good one, I am going to give it all my support, as will all clerks/practice managers, so never be afraid to put your thoughts forward. The relationship between clerk/practice manager and barrister should always be one of mutual respect, with communication going each way. You will usually find that the most successful members of the Bar are the ones who share this view.

This chapter has been looking at *pro bono* mainly as a way of enhancing your business model and your practice generally, but we should never forget the main reason for getting involved as a barrister – allowing people access to the justice they deserve, regardless of their ability to pay. By volunteering you are 'paying it forward'. My personal experience of this is that you will always get a guaranteed return – albeit as Robin Soule used to say to the barristers in his charge: "it may be in heaven Sir". I think, at worst, that is not a bad return...

About the authors

David Barnes

Chief executive and director of clerking,
Atkin Chambers
dbarnes@atkinchambers.com

David Barnes is the chief executive and director of clerking at Atkin Chambers and is a vice president of the Institute of Barristers' Clerks.

David commenced his career as a junior clerk in 1982 in the chambers of Mr Spencer G Maurice at 24 Old Buildings. In 1983 he moved to the chambers of Mr Desmond Wright QC at 22 Old Buildings, where he was to spend the next 23 years progressing from junior clerk to senior clerk in 1997. In 2006 David moved to the chambers of Richard Wilmot Smith QC and Mr Richard Davies QC at 39 Essex Chambers, where he took up the position as the first director of clerking at the Bar. In 2010 David expanded his clerking role to assume the additional role of chief executive.

During his career David has been responsible for managing, developing and expanding the practices of almost 200 barristers.

David has for many years had a great interest in the globalisation of legal services. He served as an advisory board member of the law firm management committee of the International Bar Association. His success at developing a global practice for Atkin Chambers and 39 Essex Chambers was recognised by both sets being awarded the Queen's Award for enterprise; Atkin being the first chambers to receive such an award in 2005. In 2015 David was named as the chief executive/senior clerk of the year at the inaugural *Legal 500* Awards.

David has been an active member of the Institute of Barristers' Clerks, having served its executive committee for over 10 years. In 2010 David was elected chairman, a position he held for three years. Throughout this period David was instrumental in seeking to modernise practice management at the Bar.

Chris Broom

Senior clerk, Gray's Inn Tax Chambers
cb@taxbar.com

Chris Broom has been a barristers' clerk for over 38 years, the past 20 of which he spent as senior clerk to Gray's Inn Tax Chambers.

With a proven track record of managing leading sets of barristers' chambers and the professional careers of members of the independent Bar, he carries with him the traditions of the Bar, but also embraces contemporary business practices required to organise, oversee and run the unique business model of a set of barristers' chambers. This is demonstrated in his day-to-day management style and his foresight for the future of the independent Bar. The legal directories say of him: "Chris Broom is fantastic, very social and very approachable", *Chambers and Partners* (2017 edition); "The clerking team is led by the 'brilliant' Chris Broom, who knows the business and the market", *Legal 500* (2017 edition). He is also a trustee of both the Bar *Pro Bono* Unit and Bar in the Community.

David Grief
Senior clerk, Essex Court Chambers
dgrief@essexcourt.net

With a career in managing barristers' chambers spanning over 45 years, David Grief was one of the first generation of the modern clerk and is now one of the most experienced in his field. The primary focus of David's role is to work closely with senior members of chambers to drive the business and play a key role in the strategic development of Essex Court Chambers. He is involved in and ultimately accountable for meeting all the clerking needs of every member of chambers. In addition, he provides practical support and strategic advice to each individual member in managing and developing their practices, in the United Kingdom and internationally, visiting jurisdictions of importance to chambers including Australia, Bermuda, the British Virgin Islands, the Cayman Islands, Dubai, Hong Kong, Malaysia, New York, India, Singapore, South Korea, Uganda and Zurich.

He is a regular writer and speaker on Bar management issues, marketing and business development.

Natalie Hearn
Project manager, Matrix Chambers
nataliehearn@matrixlaw.co.uk

Natalie is a project manager at Matrix Chambers and has responsibility for the monitoring and implementation of long-term and complex projects. She has managed projects relating to the creation and business development of Matrix's sister brand, Matrix International, the creation of new branding for Matrix domestically, as well as copywriting promotional material. Natalie is also the Diversity Data Officer and is responsible for our day-to-day compliance with Bar Standards Board regulations, particularly in relation to equality and diversity. She is on the E&D Committee and Management Committee of the Institute of Barristers' Clerks.

Nicholas Hill
Senior clerk, 3 New Square IP
hill@3newsquare.co.uk

Nicholas Hill has been a barristers' clerk for 30 years and a senior clerk for the last 16 years. He is currently the senior clerk at 3 New Square Intellectual Property. During his time as a senior clerk he has been awarded 'Chambers of the Year' by *Legal Week*, *The Lawyer* and *Chambers & Partners*. In addition to his chambers role, Nicholas is the chairman of the Institute of Barristers' Clerks, his three-year term started in March 2016. In this position he is a co-opted member of the Bar Council's General Management Committee. Nicholas has a particular interest in mental health; he has been a member of the Wellbeing at the Bar working group since its inception and is a regular speaker on the topic. He is a committed advocate for those with clerking and other staffing roles at the Bar to be supported in matters of wellbeing.

Christine Kings
Director, Outer Temple Chambers
christine.kings@outertemple.com

Christine Kings joined Outer Temple in 2007. Over the years she has contributed to numerous Bar initiatives particularly around pupillage recruitment, equality and diversity, and quality standards. She was chair of the Barmark panel, a member of the organising committee for the Bar Conference, and was active on Bar Council and BSB committees and working groups covering, among other things, entity regulation, public access and new business models for the Bar. Christine is a previous treasurer of the Bar *Pro Bono* Unit and trustee of Bar in the Community. She was joint chair of the Legal Practice Management Association (LPMA) until July 2017. She is a former chair of the Mary Ward Legal Centre and of Legal Action Group (LAG). In 2009 she was identified in *The Lawyer's* "Hot 100" people who made an impression on the legal profession.

Among her other roles prior to managing chambers, Christine was co-director of the Emergency Planning Information Centre. She helped set up Doughty Street Chambers in 1990 and was chief executive there until 2007.

Nicholas Luckman

Practice director, Wilberforce Chambers

nluckman@wilberforce.co.uk

Nicholas Luckman is the practice director at Wilberforce Chambers. He holds an MBA from Henley Business School and has worked in the business legal sector for over 25 years.

Nick has specialist experience in the development and delivery of agreed business strategies; maintaining and developing client relationships, as well as managing and leading teams.

In 2017, Nick wrote a paper that investigated how important gender diversity is to the survival of self-employed Bar as an independent profession. The investigation analysed the importance of retaining talent that is being lost through attrition rates amongst women barristers during their career, and considered whether the gender diversity imbalance is important to clients and the wider society.

Nick is a member the Institute of Directors, the International Bar Association and INSOL International.

Paul Martenstyn

Deputy senior clerk, Fountain Court Chambers – London & Singapore

paul@fountaincourt.co.uk

Paul Martenstyn has been a barristers' clerk since 1997. Since 2011 he has held the role of deputy senior clerk at Fountain Court Chambers, one of London's 'Magic Circle' of elite commercial chambers. Paul works alongside Fountain Court's senior clerk, Alex Taylor, the most recent (2017) edition of *The Legal 500* referring to them as the "best clerking double-act in the City". Paul is widely recognised as a thought-leader in the field of clerking: in 2007 he was the first clerk to gain a professional qualification from the Chartered Institute of Marketing, a path subsequently followed by many others, and in 2016, after two years of part-time study, Paul achieved an ILM Diploma in Leadership & Management. Paul is regularly invited to speak before a wide range of forums, which in recent times have included London's Commercial Bar Association and the International Bar Association (2017 conference, Sydney). Also in 2017, Paul was appointed as an Ambassador for Justice, the all-party law reform and human rights organisation which works to strengthen the UK justice system.

Rachel Murray

Marketing and projects assistant, Matrix Chambers

rmurray@matrixlaw.co.uk

Rachel Murray is part of the marketing and projects team at Matrix Chambers. She works alongside members to promote Matrix and is responsible for planning and delivering events, producing promotional materials, dealing with press enquiries and managing Matrix's online presence.

Amongst other marketing projects, she has worked on the launch of 'The Law of Nations' podcast series, the publication of a Matrix-led media law book and the ongoing implications of GDPR.

Rachel is an associate of the Chartered Institute of Marketing and holds a Diploma in Professional Marketing. Prior to joining Matrix in 2015, she studied English Language and Communications at King's College London.

Nick Rees
Managing director, GRL Legal LLP
nrees@grllegal.com

Nick is the managing director of GRL Legal LLP and as well as driving the business, plays an active role as a consultant.

Nick jointly created GRL in 2015 and works with many of the UK's leading barristers' chambers, law firms, innovative legal service providers and their key individuals, across recruitment, professional development, business development and consultancy projects.

His in-depth knowledge of the Bar and wider legal sector has been developed having spent more than 25 years with leading barrister chambers, law firms and as a legal consultant.

Nick's experience includes senior management roles, fee earning, mentoring of legal and non-legal staff, recruitment, project management and implementing and managing change. He has previously held positions on several Bar Council committees and similarly with the management committee of the Institute of Barristers' Clerks. Nick holds an LLB (Hons).

Felicity Schneider
Administration director, Littleton Chambers
fschneider@littletonchambers.co.uk

Felicity Schneider was born and raised in South Africa where, after completing her formal schooling, she taught school and then ran her own successful construction company. In 1995 she joined DAC Technologies, constituting her first 'real' experience of technology and its potential.

In 1999 she relocated to the United Kingdom and worked for various technology-driven organisations. She was appointed as chambers manager at Old Square Chambers in 2005 and in 2010 was headhunted to Littleton Chambers.

She is responsible for financials, human resources, general administration and IT and regulatory and compliance issues in chambers.

Felicity is acutely alive to technology as an effective enabler and has designed and driven many technology developments which effectively assist in streamlining processes, record keeping and management.

Lindsay Scott
Chief executive and director of clerking, 39 Essex Chambers
lindsay.scott@39essex.com

Lindsay Scott is chief executive and director of clerking at 39 Essex Chambers. She joined 39 Essex Chambers in November 2017, following 12 years as CEO of another leading set, and is responsible for the overall management of Chambers including developing client relationships, marketing strategy and human resources.

Lindsay, a qualified solicitor, was previously a board director of the Quarry Dougall Group and the managing director of QDOS before joining Informa plc, a FTSE 100 media and telecommunications group. She moved into legal management in 2000. In 2016 she was named "Chief Executive of the Year" at the *Legal 500* UK Awards.

Howard Sears
Partner, Price Bailey LLP
howards@pricebailey.co.uk

Howard Sears is a partner in a top 30 firm of chartered accountants, Price Bailey LLP. He is a fellow of the Chartered Institute of Certified Accountants and has specialised in looking after law firms, barristers' chambers and the professions for over 10 years.

His depth of experience and knowledge has been enhanced by his role as executive chairman of Price Bailey LLP, having been on the firm's board for 13 years.

He heads up the Price Bailey Business Team, taking responsibility for over £9 million in fees annually and a team of 90 in six locations within the South East.

Alex Taylor
Senior clerk, Fountain Court Chambers –
London & Singapore
alex@fountaincourt.co.uk

Alex started his clerking career in 1979 at Fountain Court – named John. After nine years, he moved to 11KBW as First Junior. John was Senior Clerk at Old Square Chambers for 14 years before returning to Fountain Court in 2008 as senior clerk under the name of Alex!

Alex leads and has overall responsibility for the clerking of Fountain Court Chambers. He is centrally involved in the management of Chambers as well as building and maintaining relationships with clients both domestically and internationally.

Alex received the *Legal 500* award of Senior Clerk of the Year 2018. Excellent client attention and a highly efficient bespoke clerking service have been hallmarks of Alex throughout his four-decade career. This has been recognised by the two principal legal directories, which have consistently reported on the positive impact that Alex and his team have had and the high standards of service that they deliver.

Index

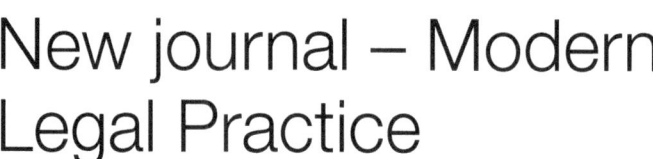

About Globe Law and Business

Globe Law and Business was established in 2005 as an imprint of Globe Business Media Group. We set out to create law books which are sufficiently high level to be of real use to the experienced professional, yet still accessible and easy to navigate. Most of our authors are drawn from Magic Circle and other top commercial firms, both in the UK and internationally.

In Autumn 2015, we had an exciting turn in our history when Globe Law and Business was bought by a management team which includes my colleague Jim Smith and me, Sian O'Neill.

We love books, and our hardback titles are carefully produced, with the utmost attention paid to the editorial, design and production processes. We hope this results in high-quality titles which are easy to read, and a pleasure to own.

Our customers and authors are of paramount importance – we are committed to devoting time and attention to each book as well as everyone involved in the publishing process.

We'd very much like to hear from you with your thoughts on our titles or ideas for improving what we offer. Please do feel free to email me on sian@globelawandbusiness.com with your views.

Sian O'Neill
Managing director
Globe Law and Business

www.globelawandbusiness.com

Related titles

Globe Law and Business

Go to **www.globelawandbusiness.com**
for full details including free sample chapters